GW00600680

Les Catt

My Life As
A Professional Gardener
For 51 Years

ISBN 978-0-9927656-5-1

Typeset in Book Antiqua 10pt

Printed by Berforts Ltd, Hastings

YouByYou Books,
Swallow Court,
High Halden Road,
Biddenden,
Kent TN27 8BD.

www.youbyyou.co.uk

Contents

Foreword

Contributed by Cllr Bruce Dowling
Mayor of Hastings

In 1973 I started working in the Hastings Parks Department. Within a short time I was accepted into a warm and welcoming team of gardeners with many years of experience between them. They dedicated themselves to improving and maintaining parks and gardens, school playing fields and other green spaces around the town. They showed a great passion for their work and met the challenges of many developments in gardening and technology over the period I worked with them.

Within the team there was Les Catt, a gardener with more than one passion in life; his work, his wife, his prose and his poetry. This book fulfils one of those passions, his work in parks and gardens. The third and fourth were sometimes combined when, on a Saturday, the local paper came out and you would often find poetry from Les to his wife within its pages. These poems always inspired positive comments at the following Monday morning tea break.

The days spent with Les and my other colleagues in parks and gardens were always interesting and amusing times to be shared and these give me great memories. I am sure that the pages of Les Catt's book will do the same for many others.

Bruce Dowling (left), with Les

Dedication

To my many workmates over the 51 years of my working life I hope you have realised my wicked sense of humour. I trust that you have realised that's what it was, as where would we be without it. Sometimes things were difficult so I think a sense of humour went a long way to alleviate the situation. Also I have been lucky in having some good mates to work with most of the time. Unfortunately some of them are not with us now, but I would like to dedicate this book to them.

Chapter One
Early Years: The Allotment and My Paper Round

When I was a young boy my big ambition was to become a professional gardener. At about the age of 10, in 1941, during the Second World War, I made my first start. I used to go with my dad to help him with his allotment. This was situated just off Frederick Road, below the gates of the old St Helen's Hospital, which isn't there anymore, and just above Valleyside Road. There was a pathway that was very long and very steep, or so it seemed to me at my young age.

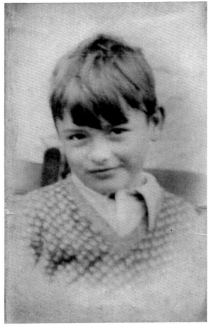

Les,
aged 10

Maybe we would spend a couple of hours or so on my dad's allotment and then hopefully return home with some produce. Actually although I used to think that I was helping I suppose really that I was just a nuisance. I spent most of my time digging holes all over the garden. My dad had the job of filling them in. When we walked home my dad said, "Thanks for your help, son." He really gave me the impression that I had helped. Of course, he was always ready with his praise. However, as I got older I began to realise that I hadn't really helped at all. I think that it was mainly because we enjoyed each other's company so much.

My dad wasn't able to go every day because he was in the Home Guard and sometimes he had to go fire-watching. In fact one night Dad and another chap had to go fire watching on the East Hill. When daylight came they found that they were right on the edge of the cliff. If they had taken another couple of steps they would have gone over the top.

I never realised that I would become a gardener for 51 years. As I still had some time to go before I left school I took a job delivering papers when I was 12 years old. I delivered about 50 papers each day for Mr Gladwish of Mount Road, for the magnificent sum of 4/- a week. I delivered the length of Victoria Avenue, Coghurst Road, Church Street (which isn't there any more), Clifton Road and Valleyside Road. We used to carry a notebook which had the list of the papers and the addresses to take them to. Unfortunately, after about two weeks I forgot to take my book with me and left it back at the shop. Apparently I didn't make any mistakes as I never heard anything any different, and I didn't have any papers left over.

After about a year Mr Gladwish asked me if I would take on another half-a-round in addition to my existing one. This would mean that I would have to deliver about another 25 papers a day for another 2/-

a week. But this meant that my new round would include Greville Road and Percy Road. This was quite a lot for me to do and get to school by 9.00.

There was a bit of comedy one morning as I walked through a passageway between Church Street and Greville Road. As I got to the front door about two or three houses into Greville Road I noticed an old boy standing in the doorway. He shouted out to me, "Come on young fella, you're late with my paper this morning."

Then I noticed he had come to the door in his long-johns so I answered him, "Yes, but I am dressed".

I had some help for a while in the shape of a little black and white dog who I called Spot. As I delivered papers down Clifton Road he used to follow me to the bottom of the road and then go back. I always called him Spot but I never got to know his name. One particular day he didn't turn up. A lady passing by said, "Oh, you haven't got your dog this morning."

I replied, "Well, he isn't my dog, he just follows me." For some reason, he didn't turn up again. I was quite worried about him as I had got attached to him over several months. After a while I could only assume that his owners had moved away. At least that is what I hoped, as I never saw him again.

Les, aged 12

9

Ellen Frances Catt, Les's mother, aged about 20 in 1914

Albert Leonard Catt, aged about 22

The Second World War in Hastings

Notes written by Les in a Woolworth's notebook after the war.

July 26th 1940 until the end of the war Hastings had 85 visits in air raids. 154 were killed, 260 had various serious injuries and 439 had lesser injuries. Last flying bomb was on August 28th 1944.

A total of 550 H.E. bombs and 15 flying bombs, 12 incendiary bombs and 750 smaller incendiary bombs. 463 houses were demolished and 14,818 houses damaged.

The London Blitz was from September 1940 until May 1941. On Thursday August 15th 50-60 planes flew up the Channel. On Thursday September 12th, 15 High Explosives and 150 incendiaries were dropped in the Clive Vale area.

Saturday September 14th: a stick of 9 bombs fell in a line up All Saints Street and High Wickham but they didn't explode. Gas holders in Queen's Road were holed and set alight. Ray Grant, a 26-year-old employee of Southern Railway and a member of the Home Guard, helped to plug holes with clay. Then, unaided, he plugged up another hole, with flames pouring out of an adjacent holder. Although in great danger he worked for half an hour until he had plugged the hole. He received the George Medal.

On Wednesday September 11th 14,000 evacuees left by train and 5,000 by special coaches.

On Tuesday April 8th Municipal Hospital was bombed at night. 28 H.E.S. and 300 incendiaries. 2 nurses were injured. One nurse, Dorothy Gardner, flung herself across a patient as masonry fell on them. She suffered severe head injuries and was in hospital for months. She was awarded the George Medal.

Invasion danger was in March 1941.

Sunday May 3rd: bombs fell in Ore. 2 sisters were buried in their shop.

Rationing

January 8th 1940 rationing began:- bacon, ham, sugar, and butter.
March 1940:- meat rationed
July 1940:- tea, margarine, cooking fats and cheese
March 1941:- jam, marmalade, treacle and syrup
June 1941:- eggs controlled
August 1941:- extra cheese ration for manual workers
November 1941:- milk controlled
December 1941:- national dried milk controlled
January 1942:- rice and dried fruit controlled
February 1942:- canned peas and tomatoes controlled
April 1942:- cereals and condensed milk controlled
June 1942:- American dried egg powder for sale
July 1942:- sweets rationed
August 1942:- biscuits controlled
December 1942:- oat flakes controlled
December 1944:- extra tea for over 70s
January 1945:- whale meat for sale
July 1946:- bread rationed

My brother and I had a lucky escape one morning during the war when we lived in Sandown Road in Ore village. We were only about 8 and 9 years old. We heard this plane coming and we rushed home from Oakfield Road which is the next road to Sandown. As we got within sight of our house a German plane started machine gunning us. Fortunately we didn't get hurt but a man standing at his front door in Oakfield Road was shot through the hand.

Chapter Two
First Gardening Job: St. Helens

When I was coming up to 14 years of age in 1945 I managed to find myself a gardening job in the St. Helens area. In those days we left school at 14. As my birthday came in the Easter holidays, I worked all day Saturdays for seven hours a day at 8d an hour. There was another boy, Eric, who worked there and he was about 18 months older than me. An old lady and gentleman lived there.

The old chap had a tailor's business in Savile Row in London. So most of the time the old lady lived there on her own during the week.

It was a big garden and there was plenty to do. One of our first jobs when we were both there together was to get rid of the barbed wire. That was quite a tricky job as it was so difficult to handle. It had been placed along the lane on the outside of the premises to keep people out during the war. Now the war had finished we could dispense with this. I suppose it took us about a week to get rid of it.

We had just about finished this particular job when there was such a commotion just outside the door leading out of the garden into the lane. Suddenly this heavy door burst open and about half a dozen youngsters came bursting in. They only seemed a little older than ourselves. They were actually German prisoners-of-war. They had come down from a working party at the Records Office which was in Elphinstone Road just below Hastings cemetery. They were certainly very noisy with their chattering but of course we couldn't understand one another very well. They did quite a lot of laughing but neither Eric nor I were able to understand them. Anyway, we were pleased to get the job of rolling up the barbed wire out of the way.

At this time, 1945-6, when I went to the Hastings cemetery by bus there were usually some Land Girls on it. I think they were working down Pine Avenue somewhere.

One day the old lady who owned the house came out in the garden and asked me if I would take a letter across the road to Jack as she wanted him to come over and do some work for her. I said of course I would. He was a bricklayer and at the present time he was working on the opposite side of the lane at the St. John's Nursing Home. So I walked across the lane and when I looked up to see where he was, he was on some scaffolding about three floors up.

I called out to him that I had got a letter for him from my boss, and that she wanted him to do some work at our place.

"Okay Les, bring it up please," he called to me.

"Oh, I don't know about that, Jack, as I've got no head for heights, " I replied.

"Oh, you'll be alright, Les," he called down.

So, I started up to the first floor. That was alright but of course as I went higher I began to get a bit shaky. He called out to me, "That's right, Les, you're nearly here". As I went even higher I felt even shakier. Really this was as high as I wanted to go. So, after a bit of a blow and Jack telling me that I was nearly there I gradually pressed on and I eventually got to the 3rd floor. I did feel quite proud of myself. However, I didn't intend to hang about. I just handed over the letter and started back down.

"Thanks Les, you've done very well," said Jack.

I slowly went down to *terra firma*. When I got to ground level I was really shaking and I took my time in getting over to the other side of the lane. I walked very slowly until I had stopped shaking.

This reminds me of when I lived in Sandown Road in Ore Village when the builders were working there. They had put a ladder up to the roof from our back yard. They usually put a board up so that no cats could get on the roof. Anyway, this particular time they hadn't bothered and apparently there was a cat already on the roof. So I went up the ladder and encouraged the cat to come to me. I was pleased to see that it was a small cat and I was able to grab him with one hand and take him down the ladder.

In the summer months when it was quite hot in the garden at St. Helens we used to get a lot of snakes, mostly grass snakes. The old lady used to have a nasty habit of blowing a whistle when she wanted us for anything. This was quite annoying, as you can imagine. However, then we found out that the old lady didn't like snakes and she was prepared to give us a 1/- for every one she was shown by us. But I'm afraid that we were rather naughty. It seems that the snakes were very prevalent and several shillings used to be going into our pockets. Anyway, we told her that the reason that there were so many snakes about was that they were attracted to her whistle. It seemed to do the trick as she didn't blow her whistle so often after that, about which we were very pleased.

We were gradually making inroads into the rubbish in the garden. As it was dark when we finished work at 4.30 and there were no lights at all in the lane, it was tricky to get up to the ridge.

One particular afternoon, as I made my way up in the dark, I got almost to the top of the lane when I saw a big pair of eyes coming towards me. I didn't know whether to turn round and run back down the lane or keep going. I decided to keep going and as I gradually got nearer these eyes seemed to get bigger until suddenly I could see what it was: a cow. I should think that it must have got out from somewhere.

I expect most people think gardening is a piece of cake, so to speak. However I can assure them that there is a very great deal to learn and much more than I would have thought when I first started. Now, with 51 years experience behind me, I have seen most aspects of it at first hand and I now have a true picture.

As to the work that my mate and I were doing in the garden at St. Helens, we realised that we wouldn't be able to tame it alone. This was a garden that had been let run riot during the war years. All we had managed to do between us was to get the worst of the rubbish cut down and burnt, and also when the weather was rainy, to tidy up the greenhouse. To start with we had a job to get into the greenhouse because of the amount of rubbish. We gradually got it all cleared out, though we saved this job we saved for rainy days. We had to be out clearing the garden as much as possible.

We were very pleased when an older man started to work with us. He was probably between 30 and 35. Obviously he knew much more about gardening than we did together. He gradually got the garden organised by doing one area at a time. I think we were trying to get it all organised at the same time which of course was impossible.

When we had got part of the greenhouse reasonably tidy we got some seed trays and planted tomato seeds in them. Then, when we had tidied the rest of the greenhouse we prepared the thumb pots for the individual plants. The next rainy day we would concentrate on planting the rest of the tomato seeds.

We had a good spell of weather so we cleared most of the kitchen garden and burned up the rubbish. Then we arranged for a load of manure to be dumped on one of the areas which was designated for the tomatoes. We took out a trench at the top of this piece of ground and threw the soil into the barrow to wheel it down to the bottom. Then we dug the ground over in the first trench and put the manure in it. We continued until the last trench was filled in. It took us about three days but it was worth it because when the tomatoes had grown in the greenhouse we would be able to plant them outside.

We had got the garden fairly tidy by now. One of the next jobs was to clear the orchard out which was in a terrible mess. A few days later our foreman asked me if I could use a swop as a couple of us would be cutting the grass and brambles down in the orchard.

In the meantime when we had a wet day we concentrated on getting the tomato seeds potted up so within about two weeks they would be ready to be planted out, which we were very pleased about.

Then they would need quite a lot of looking after. When we got them all planted outside we had to tie them up to stakes, picking off all the side shoots every day.

When we tied them up we had to make sure to do it in the correct way. This was in a figure of eight, meaning that the tie had to be made to the cane and not the plant. If it was tied in this way it would cut into the plant. Also now they were planted out they would want plenty of water. I think this could be the most awkward part really because in those days, in the 1940s, we didn't have such things as hose pipes. All the water had to be brought down to the kitchen garden by a bowser which was like a bath. It had to be filled up in the kitchen with water cans and then brought down. It was a very slow process as altogether we had planted about 550 plants. As you can imagine it took a long time as we had to have several lots of water. When we got the bowser to where the plants were it was a question of watering with a can. We had to do this about every other day.

But what with the manure and the watering they soon started growing. In fact in just over two months we were picking them.

The Jesuits (who now have a place on the Ridge called Friary Gardens) used to have some of our tomatoes. They would phone our people to arrange when they were coming. We used to pick the tomatoes and they would call by for them. To start with we only had a few pounds but, after a while, with 550 plants, we were picking many pounds at least twice a week. So we felt proud of the way things were going.

Now we made a start on getting the orchard tidy as the Jesuit priests would be coming down and picking the fruit themselves. Apparently they gave a price on the tree before it was picked and when the time arrived they just came and picked them. Mind you, they wouldn't have been able to pick the fruit at the start as they wouldn't have been able to even get into the orchard. There were two of us cutting down the grass but it was in such a mess we knew that it would take a while. Actually it took about four days. Then we started clearing all the rubbish and had a fire going to burn it all up. Within about another three days it was clear for them to pick the fruit.

One of my regular jobs every morning, after we had finished our 10.00 lunch, was to take a barrow of logs across the terrace, put them inside the French windows and then place them each side of the fireplace. Also I had to get some coal and the cellar was quite near to the terrace. One morning I was down in the cellar and I heard the door being bolted from the outside. So I rushed up the stairs and hammered on the door. The old lady called out, "Is that you Leslie?" So I let her know that it was and that I didn't fancy being locked up in the cellar for goodness knows how long. I really didn't like the prospect of it at all.

Now that the weather was pretty dodgy we got the 30 foot long shed ready to cut up the wood. There was never going to be any prospect of running out of firewood as there were plenty of woods within the 20 acres of land which belonged to this house. One day there was one quite big tree which had to be cut down in the meadow. We had to use a cross-cut saw on that one. Of course neither of us had ever used a cross-cut saw before so this was interesting. The foreman and the older boy started it off at first until it was felled, then I was able to have a turn. It was quite difficult to get used to, because you tended to want to push the saw instead of just pulling it towards you. Then when the tree was felled we had to saw it up into pieces that were the right size for carrying up to the shed which was about a hundred yards away. When we had sawn it up into pieces to take up to the shed it had to be split up with wedges. I had quite a lot of branches to carry up and I suppose that we were lucky that the weather was favourable to us so that we got the whole lot in the shed while the rain kept away. Unfortunately it wasn't so good the next day and it was a shed day. So we were able to cut up the pieces of wood which needed splitting up with wedges.

The next day was a Friday and we tried to tidy up around the house as much as possible for the weekend.

We also gave some time to the tomatoes as they now needed to be picked about every other day. Also the foreman and the other boy were starting to prune the soft fruit bushes such as black and red currants, gooseberries, etc. I was kept very busy trying to keep the weeds down and burning them up including all the cuttings from the pruning. We were gradually beginning to make a clearance now, but there had been so much rubbish. I knew that it was a process that would take a long time.

Now that the kitchen garden was reasonable we could begin to branch out and do other jobs. As you walked across the terrace there was a big conservatory. A large acacia tree had literally grown through the roof. It must have taken a long time to do that. Going through the conservatory there was a flight of steps down to a gravel path. There was a small lawn and flower border around it. But over on the left of this there was a long drive. It was hard to tell whether it was a gravel drive or not as it was so overgrown, and we decided to leave it till last.

We spent a couple of days each week in the vegetable garden and the other 3½ days starting to clear up the areas which were still overgrown. Of course one problem was that we had to take the rubbish down to the vegetable garden to burn it as it would have been too close to the house.

As well as the drive there was a large area of grass which stretched from the wall below the terrace to the bottom of the drive. So two of us started to cut all this grass down which we realised would take a long time. Anyway we managed to cut about half of it and raked it up ready to burn near the bottom of the lawn. Then we took the rest of the rubbish from the drive down to the vegetable garden to burn.

The next week was more-or-less a repeat performance which was a good thing as we could see that we were making good progress, now that we had some sort of plan.

After our session on the kitchen garden we came back to the front drive again and cleared the rest of the rubbish. Also the grass bank which we had half done, we completed, cutting that down and taking it to the vegetable garden to burn. So now most of the garden was reasonable. However there was a gravel path or I assume it was, as it was rather a job to tell as it was absolutely thick with rubbish. We carried on clearing the rubbish, burning it in the kitchen garden and then starting our round again.

Now came the worst part of the garden to work on, the gravel pathway from just below the terrace. We had to chop it out in large lumps. Just around the corner where the pathway to the vegetable garden started, there was an old and very much extinct swimming pool. As there was already plenty of rubbish there we thought an extra lot wouldn't be out of place. As we could see that there would be many barrows of rubbish all three of us concentrated on this one job to get it done. So I became the barrow boy, taking the rubbish away while the other two filled up the barrows.

One Tuesday night when I walked up to my bus stop outside the Hastings Cemetery we had some rain which was very cold. In fact it froze on the tram lines as the buses ran off overhead wires at the time. This was in 1947. So it meant that I should have to walk home which wasn't very nice. For one thing it wasn't easy walking as it was very slippery. I suppose the distance was about a couple of miles but as walking was rather difficult it seemed farther. Also it meant that I would be walking to and fro for a few days. I was pleased that we were more-or-less up to date now with the work on the gardens. As it was we had plenty of inside work to do. I know that it was only cutting up wood but at least we had got a good store in our nice big shed of 30ft long or thereabouts.

The old lane that I walked down was made all the worse because the bad weather had brought quite a lot of trees down. It took almost twice as long to get anywhere. So we went into 1948 hoping things would be better, and thankfully this weather didn't last very long.

However I had been doing some serious thinking about the workforce. Now that the garden was tidier I was wondering whether there was going to be enough work for the three of us. So I made up my mind to keep my eyes and ears open. Of course I had got to know a few people in gardening by now so I was quite hopeful. After about a couple of weeks I heard a whisper about a possible job in Lower Park Road, near the park, at a nursing home. I didn't waste any time and when I got the chance I made my way there. There was already a gardener there but unfortunately he was so tied up with doing jobs indoors that he didn't get much chance to get out in the garden.

When he asked me my name and I told him that it was Les Catt he said, "Are you any relation to Bert Catt?" and when I replied that I was his youngest son, he said, "Well I never, I have known your dad for years. If you are interested in working here I must warn you that it's in a pretty bad state".

He wasn't joking. I think it was probably a good job that I had spent about 2½ years in a garden that was so untidy. However, I never expected to find one that was in a worse state. The best way that I can describe it was that it was like a rubbish dump. My previous experience would stand me in good stead. I couldn't think when was the last time that anybody had done any gardening there. The money was also a little bit better than at St. Helens. So I said that I would make a start in two weeks' time, after which I said my goodbyes to my mates and the lady of the house, who gave me a good reference.

Les, 16, and his mother walking along Robertson Street, 1947

Chapter Three
Lower Park Road

In my new job at the nursing home in Lower Park Road my hours were better than at St. Helens, in so far as I would have an extra half hour for dinner so I would be able to go home. The only thing was that I didn't have a watch. However if I looked across the park I could see the time by Blacklands Church clock. So on the Monday morning when I got to Keynor House, the nursing home, I was met by Fred, the head gardener. He showed me around and where the tools were kept.

Then I said to him, "Can I suggest that I clear a space on this piece of ground, enough to make a fire and then start tidying up the front first?"

"That's a good idea Les, you'll find that I won't interfere with what work you are doing, but to start with I expect that I shall see you most mornings."

Anyway, on the first day I got there at 8.00 and found the tools I needed which were just a spade and a fork. I cleared a small patch for when I would have a fire. Of course I didn't start burning it until the following day. I think there were five flower beds on a lawn at the front of the house, all of which were overgrown. I was pleased that the shears worked pretty well, both edging and hand shears. I thought that I would get one flower bed completed at a time. So I edged round the first one and carried the rubbish up to the back garden. When I arrived, there was a cup of tea for me, which went down rather well. I carried on clearing the first flower bed and I had quite a battle to clear out the weeds. However I was beginning to get some of it done. By the time I took the third lot of rubbish up to the back garden I looked across at Blacklands Church clock and saw it was 11.50, just 10 minutes to the time when I would leave to walk through the park and up to Langham pub to catch my bus. It was quite nice to be able to get home to dinner. I got back at 1.30 to make another start on what I was hoping one day would look like a garden. I'd found a swop up in the shed so I was able to cut the lawn grass which I hoped would soon look like a lawn. Then I raked up the grass and took it to the fire area.

The next morning when I saw Fred I said to him, "Now that I have cut the grass roughly where the lawn is with a swop, what about us getting a hand mower to keep the grass fairly short?"

"Yes of course, you are quite right Les, that's what we must do now."

Fred told me a couple of days later that the hand mower had arrived. I was able to roughly mow the lawn at the front. Of course it would be mowed better the more often it was mowed. So after three days I had got the front lawn roughly mowed and one flower bed almost weeded. The next morning I got a fire going first and cleared a bit more near the fire, making more room to move about.

Then I concentrated on tidying up the first flower bed and digging it over. I carried on clearing the weeds out of the second flower bed, but it didn't show how much yet as it was in such a state. By the end of the week I had roughly weeded and dug over two flower beds. I knew it was going to be a slow business because of the state of the garden but I was satisfied with how the work was going. The next week I cleared a bigger area at the back of the garden so I could have a bigger fire. Then onto the flower beds again and I could begin to see some daylight at last.

By the end of the second week I was getting into the spirit of things. So on the Friday I could see that the front lawn and the flower beds were looking smarter day by day. I know it was pretty repetitive but we were getting somewhere at last. The next week I concentrated on making the front lawns and flower beds tidy. One day when I went home to dinner I must have read the church clock wrong as I seemed to have got home very early. Anyway when I saw Fred the next morning he spoke to me about it. He said that I went home early the day before, half an hour early.

"Yes I realised that when I got home," I said to him. "I must have misread the church clock."

"Well," he said, "you could have come back half an hour earlier to make up for it."

"Yes, you are absolutely right Fred, that's what I should have done. I'm so sorry about that, but I'll work an extra half hour in the afternoon to make up for it. I don't think that it's likely to happen again as I intend to buy myself a pocket watch at the weekend."

"Don't worry about making up the half hour as it was just a mistake."

So I bought my pocket watch at the weekend and that solved being able to keep the time.

The next week when I saw Fred on the Monday morning he told me that the next job would be the orchard. It was difficult to imagine that there were about two dozen fruit trees in there as they were covered in brambles.

"Will you give me a free hand to do it my way?"

"Of course I will, you seem to be doing very well so far."

So first of all I cleared quite a piece of ground to have the fire on. Then as the front garden was pretty good I spent a couple of days clearing the area leading up to what should have been the vegetable garden. It wasn't a big area, but like the rest of the garden it was very rubbishy.

Then on the Thursday morning I got the fire going

28

and burnt all the rubbish because on Fridays I liked the front to be nice and tidy.

On the next Monday I started to carve my way into the so-called orchard. Now I had to put my efforts into keeping the rubbish burnt up. There certainly was plenty of it. I gradually worked my way into the orchard and cut up the rubbish as I went so that it was ready to burn. This took about another week. Now that most of it was cut up I could see that we were getting somewhere. There was one more bad patch on the right of the orchard. This was covered in a very fast and obnoxiously growing weed called marestail.

We were now into another year. Apart from the awful marestail, most of the time I was just going round from the front lawn to the rest of the garden to keep it all tidy.

One day in July I had a nasty shock in the post. It was a letter which informed me to report to Oswestry army camp on Thursday July 21st 1949 by 4.00 in the afternoon, for 18 months' military training. I shouldn't have been shocked as I was expecting it. I told Fred about it the next day and I said that I would work until Friday 15th. This would give me a few days' rest before I had to go.

He said, "Well, we are very pleased with the tremendous amount of work you have done". When I left there and they all said cheerio to me, Fred gave me an extra packet containing another week's money. In a way I was sorry to be leaving there. I certainly didn't relish the prospect of doing my military training but, like everything in life, it had to be faced.

Chapter Four
Army Days

On July 21st 1949 I left home about 4.00 in the morning, ready to walk to Ore railway station. My dad came down with me. I wasn't looking forward to the train journey as I realised how long it must be, and the furthest I had ever travelled by train had been to Brighton. Anyway it wasn't too bad up to London and then we had to change trains. When we got on the other train we realised that there were a lot of young men on it, who were probably going to Oswestry training camp, the same as I was. Some of us got talking and we realised that this was so.

It was about half past three when we eventually got there. There were several army lorries waiting for us to take us to the camp. It was quite a scramble but after a while we were on our way. Not that it was something to look forward to. What *was* something to look forward to was a nice cup of tea and something to eat. After the journey I felt that I could eat a doormat if it was well cooked. Of course I kept this to myself as if I had said it out loud they may have taken me up on it. Apparently there were about 6,000 troops in the camp but it seemed many more to me, considering that I was used to either working on my own or with two or three other people at the most. When we had some tea and something to eat I managed to feel a bit better.

The next step was to be fitted out with our boots and uniforms. That was quite a scramble as you can imagine, especially with some people who didn't seem to know their size. After about two hours we finally got things sorted out. Then we were shown to our billets.

By this time it was getting quite late in the evening. As this had been such a long, drawn-out day I think all most of us wanted to do was to have a lie down. Surprise, surprise, the beds were there but they hadn't been made up for us. There was just the bedstead and the bed clothes in a heap on top. It really would look as though we were going to have to make the beds ourselves. Not that I minded as before I started to go to work at 14 years old I always used to help my mum make the beds.

Maybe I had a bit of a doze, but I don't think I actually went to sleep. The next morning about 5.30 there was a terrible crashing on the bottom rail of our bedsteads. First of all I thought the end of the world had come. Then we heard the roar of an N.C.O. or a bombardier telling us to get up. I must admit that I didn't think this was a very nice way to inform us. He told us where the cook house was, which was one item of good news. Also he told us to be outside on parade at 8.30.

So we all got outside and lined up in some sort of order. Then a sergeant who we found out was the orderly sergeant came along the line asking various questions. This was to find out if we had any preference for what we wanted to do. One of the chaps said that he would prefer to be an ex-serviceman. Of course this didn't go down very well. No, it wasn't me.

After about half an hour of this we were marched - I think that was what they called it - down to the gun store to get a rifle each. Then we were given some instructions on rifle drill, though some of us hardly knew which end was which. We eventually sorted things out and did some sort of rifle drill. I don't know what our particular brand was called but I do think that it began to grow on us. We used to do marching and rifle drill for about two hours each morning which we found very tiring, because we weren't used to it. Then instead of easing off, it continued into the afternoon as well. We did gradually get better at it. I think the worst part was during the morning when we were going through with the marching rifle drill, we were told to fall out for a break. Of course there was a rush to the naafi and the ones who were nearest were quickly served, but anyone who was somewhere at the back, by the time they got to the counter the call went up, "Outside now, on parade!" Of course it's like everything else, I suppose you get used to it.

As well as the inevitable marching and rifle drill we also had a couple of sessions in the gym each week. We were only supposed to be stationed at Oswestry for a couple of weeks just for us to get used to army life. Near the gym there was a railway line and trains seemed to run through there quite frequently. When my two weeks were finished I got a posting to a signal regiment at Kimnel Park near Rhyl in North Wales. Five of us were posted there so at least we would know four other people.

It was roughly the same sort of situation as Oswestry. On the first morning we went out on parade and we were asked if we had any preference in what we wanted to do. We split up into pairs and each pair carried a great big wireless set all over the place. We were glad to get back to camp and rest our tired limbs.

We were supposed to stay in Kimnel Park for eight weeks. Anyway I was quite surprised when they asked if any of us wanted a 48-hour pass the following weekend. We could leave the camp on Friday evening and get back on Monday morning. I soon put in for it the following week. Of course I wasn't able to let my mum and dad know. So I had to arrive home in Hastings without telling them I was coming. No doubt we would be pleased to see one another. So I was looking forward to the next weekend. It was a lot of travelling for a short time at home but I felt that it would be worth it.

On Friday about 6.00 in the evening I was away, down to London. Then I got a train right through to Hastings. It was so good to see Hastings again, even though I had only been away for a few weeks. While I was travelling on the last part of the journey I felt that the bus couldn't get me there quick enough. As I knocked on the front door my mum came to answer it. As she opened the door I said, "Have you got room for a soldier?"

"Oh, it's Les!" she said, and my dad was soon at the door as well.

I said that I wasn't able to let them know but I thought that they wouldn't mind putting me up for a couple of nights: "I'm sorry that it won't be very long as I have only got a 48-hour pass." However it was very nice to be able to get out and about around the town before I forgot what it looked like. We all three went to the park on the Saturday. Also we had plenty of time to go to various places together where we hadn't been for some time. Of course the time went all too quickly and before we realised it Monday morning had come round. So I said my goodbyes to my mum and dad and said how nice it was to be home and to see them again. Also, that the next time I should be having a longer leave, probably seven days, and I hoped it would be soon.

So I set out to Hastings station and caught the train to London. Then I got on another train that took me back to Rhyl. I know that it was a very long journey but I felt that it was certainly worth it.

***

While I was at Kimnel Park we used to have sessions in the gym. I was quite terrified one morning when I went in there. They had a boxing ring rigged up. Apparently they would pick out a couple of us who were round about the same weight. It didn't seem to matter whether you could box or not. I must admit that I didn't have a clue. My name was called out and as I was making my way towards the ring one of the chaps at the ringside said, "You want to watch this chap, Les, he is an amateur boxer."

I replied, "Oh that's just great. It should be interesting, especially for me."

We squared up to one another, if that is the right expression. Without me even saying anything to upset him he started hitting me. But he didn't seem to stop. In fact I think the referee must have been helping him as I was being hit from so many angles. I didn't think it possible that the same person was hitting me all the time. It wasn't as though I said anything to offend him. I did wish him luck at the start of the contest. I began to wish I hadn't.

***

I was only at Kimnel Park at Rhyl for my eight weeks' signalling training when I got a posting to Plymouth. This was a school of artillery and we found out after a little while that officers and sergeants used to come there on courses. We gunners were only to make the numbers up. The place where we used to have our coast defence guns was a place called Lentney which was about seven miles from Plymouth.

Mostly they were six inch guns and the shells weighed one hundred pounds each. We had to load the shell in the breach, which took two men. One man lifted it into the breach and then turned round and, assisted by another man, together they used a rammer to ram it into the barrel of the gun. The next thing another man handed up a charge which was below the gun floor and was handed up to be put in with the shell. Then it was fired by a lanyard. If things weren't done properly it could be very dangerous. When the gun was fired the breach of the gun used to come back about 18 inches so you had to be aware of these things and keep well back.

When the officers or sergeants were on a gun shift us mere gunners had to get the shells ready for them. The ammunition was in a place underground which meant carrying these heavy shells up about twenty steps. There were usually about four or five of us on this. It was a good job we didn't have to carry them far to the gun floor from the top of the underground store.

We didn't fire many rounds in any one day, thank goodness. The charges were quite easy, they only weighed about 11 pounds each. The only thing to remember was that the charges had to be put in a compartment under the gun floor which had steel doors. It wouldn't have been a very good idea leaving the charges out in the open before the gun had been fired. Otherwise they would most probably have ignited and blown up the gun and all the people around about as well.

One night I went out on a launch with two others. That was a bombardier and another gunner as well as myself. We were going along quite merrily on the launch when from the shore all hell broke loose. The gun layers on the shore seemed to be lined up on our launch instead of the target which we were towing. Our bombardier called up the shore on the radio and said to them: "Would you mind laying on the target which we were towing instead of the launch?" So they apologised and did just that, which made us feel a whole lot safer. It certainly was quite a frightening experience as the target wasn't very far behind our launch. All I can say is that it was a good job the gun layers weren't very good or accurate or we would have been in trouble.

Back at the camp at Plymouth we used to have what we called a dummy loader. We used to practice with dummy shells which was heavy work because although we only used dummy shells they weighed exactly the same. It had to be that way otherwise we wouldn't have the true picture when we actually fired the real things. We were really the dogsbodies who carried out the donkey work. One of the worst jobs was when we had a delivery of shells to take down to the gun store. Descending the 20 steps carrying the heavy weight used to catch you in the legs.

Back at the camp about half a dozen of us were picked out to train on a dummy loader. We used to have two shifts of about half an hour at a time. Then we would hand over to the other lot. We used to do two lots like that and believe me that's all you needed. After two half-hour sessions you had just about had enough for one day.

Sometimes at Lentney where the guns were situated we used quite a bit of 'skidding' (blocks of wood), moving the smaller guns around. I couldn't see the sense of it myself. Why move guns around which were meant to be static? The skidding that we used were two different sizes. They were both a foot square but one lot were six foot in length; it took six of us to carry just one as they were solid. The four foot ones could be carried by four people. We couldn't see the reasoning behind it but we didn't need to know, but just to get on and do it.

Round about that time there was a rumour going around that there were saboteurs about, so we had to put a night guard on patrolling the area where the guns were. We used to be taken out there by army lorry and picked up the next morning. This guard was from four o'clock in the afternoon until eight o'clock the next morning, at the time of year when it was getting darker in the autumn. I suppose what with carrying the 100lbs shells around and now carrying this skidding around as well it built our muscles up, not that we enjoyed it much. Mind you, they were a good crowd of chaps and we worked well together so we couldn't grumble. This seemed to go on for a few weeks and then it seemed to fizzle out. Talking it over amongst ourselves we wondered what bright ideas they would think of next.

One thing we did miss was that while we were doing guards here we didn't do them back at camp. When we talked it over we said that we bet we should be grabbed to do guards soon after we got back to camp. Of course we had been comparatively lucky in that respect that when we got back to camp after being on guard at Lentney we had a free hand to do what we liked, within reason. Certainly no duties at camp for the time being, anyhow. Mind you, we still had our share of marching and rifle drill.

It was getting quite late in the year now and of course we were thinking about getting home for Christmas, maybe seven days' leave this time. I checked that I would be able to get home first and then wrote to my mum and dad that I would be home for seven days including Christmas Day and Boxing Day. I had a letter back within a few days from my mum and dad saying how pleased they were to hear the news and that they were looking forward to welcoming me home, once again. But of course as it is with everything the more you look forward to a thing the more it seems to drag.

It came round at last and when I got home this time my mum and dad were more prepared. We got out and about quite a lot during the week and the time went very quickly and, like all good things, it came to an end. Both my mum and dad were sorry to see me leave to get back to the army camp at Plymouth. But as I said to them, "Never mind, it's about another year now and then it will all be finished". Not like my dad, who had to serve for four years in the 1914-18 war.

We got through the winter into the spring and we started to go out for runs in the morning. I remember one day we went out on a five mile run. It was alright for the sergeant who was taking us, as he was riding a bike. After about a mile and a half my foot had become so sore and when I took my boot and sock off I saw that I had a nasty blister on my heel. The sergeant got off his bike and said, "It would be a good idea if you waited here until we come back as we'll be returning this way."

I replied, "Well thanks for the offer Sarge, but I'll be alright."

"Well, it's up to you Gunner but the offer is there."

Mind you, the next couple of miles made the blister a whole lot worse but I managed to grit my teeth a bit harder and eventually we got back to camp. Believe me, I don't think that I'd ever been so pleased to see the barracks.

Later on in the spring, we had a sports day at the camp. We called it 'potted' sports but in one way it was more like potty sports. We were split into four sections and each person had to have a go at three different sports. As I was no good at sprinting I thought the longer distance would be better for me. When I went for the mile it certainly seemed a long way but in no way was I an athlete. I just jogged along but I only came in fourth.

Another one that I went in for was rather peculiar and consisted of crawling underneath some sheets of canvas. The trouble was that it was so dark in there that it was difficult to get your bearings and almost impossible to know whether you were going in the right direction or not. I felt sure that they would soon send someone in to look for me. Eventually I got out and I was rather surprised that the others were still there. I visualised that they must have packed up and gone back to camp by now. I asked with tongue-in-cheek if I had won it, but I hadn't.

Now I was faced with my last item of sport which was certainly different. It was throwing a cricket ball. It seems that my sense of direction wasn't very good. I threw what I thought was a good throw but it went over someone's hedge. I expected to see someone stick their head up over the hedge with a bump on their head, like we tend to see in cartoons.

I was getting to know a few of the chaps now, and one in particular called Louie Wonacott. I must admit that he used to go out for a few drinks in the evening, and I know it was his money, but I'm afraid that he was too good about buying everyone drinks.

Very often he used to ask me if I could let him have some polish or cleaning material. Of course I never did refuse because he was thoughtful in helping other people. One night I found that I was on guard duty with him and he was such good company. I never used to sleep on guard duty but most of the chaps did. I could never doze off for a short time like some people do. So my first port of call was to go around to the billets and shout out, "Come on now, it's 11.00, lights out!" The chaps were quite reasonable about it.

What used to be worse, some of the fellows used to come to the guard room the night before and put in for you to give them an early call for the next morning. That was alright, providing that it was genuine, but with one or two of them they thought it was a good joke. But when we called them early we had to get a signature in the book to say that we had called them. Sometimes they used to get quite nasty about it. I could understand how they felt. Say for instance that they were called at 5.00 instead of 6.00, it was understandable to get a bit peeved. At 11.00 we had to turn off the outside lights. This was in the married quarters at Plymouth.

Sometimes when we were on guard we might ask one of our mates to get a couple of Cornish pasties for us. They were so tasty and we weren't able to get them ourselves.

As I say I became a good mate with Louie. He had been in the army about six months longer than me. Like myself he didn't like it very much and was looking forward to getting out. He said to me one morning, "Have you read the latest news, Les? They are talking about extending 18 months to two years." He was banking on leaving after 18 months and I think that he only had about three or four months left.

I don't think it was when I had been on guard but one morning one of the chaps in our billet said to me, "Oh Les, you weren't half snoring last night."

"I'm sorry," I said, "why didn't you wake me up?"

"Wake you up?" he said. "Three of us tried to."

There were, I think, eight beds each side of the barrack room, making 16 altogether. One morning when I woke up I found my bed had been let down. Mind you, it didn't wake me up.

While I was stationed at Plymouth we had a visit from Princess Elizabeth who came into an area called the Barbican, by boat. She was still Princess Elizabeth at that time as this was about 1950 or 1951. We fired a 21 gun salute from the ramparts of the Royal Citadel. We used four 25 pounder guns, firing at five second intervals. We did hit one snag and that was that we had a misfire on one of the guns. So we finished the 21 gun salute with only three guns.

My mate Louie lived quite near Plymouth - that is if you can call 20 miles near - in a town called

Kingsbridge. He used to try to get home when he wasn't on duty on a Wednesday. One Wednesday he asked me to go home with him. He had already asked his mum and dad and they had agreed. Of course it would be by Shanks's pony and we might have to do quite a lot of walking. I didn't mind that as I have always been quite a good walker. But as it was, of course, we were in uniform. Then a car pulled up and a chap in civvies asked us where we were heading. When we told him Kingsbridge he said, "Well, you are lucky because that's just where I am going. You are from the camp at the Citadel aren't you?"

When we said that we were he added, "That's where I'm from, I am an officer there". So he took us all the way to Kingsbridge and we thanked him very much and he shook hands with both of us.

So then I met Louie's mum and dad who seemed very pleased to meet me and of course I was very pleased to meet them. I suppose we spent about three hours with them and then we left to walk back. We weren't so lucky this time and felt quite tired when we got back to the camp. Never mind, I felt that it was well worth it.

A few days later Louie said to me again that the 18 months' national service was to be extended to two years. What made it worse for him was that it was due to start two weeks before he was due to finish his 18 months' service. It was an understatement to say that he was rather annoyed. Anyway, we carried on much as before, just wishing that the time would go.

One day Louie and I walked across the Hoe when the weather was nice. There were a lot of very tall monuments there, some of them were about 100ft high. He suggested that we went up one of them, but I didn't have any head for heights.

Anyway, to cheer him up a bit I agreed to go. There were certainly a lot of stairs, but when we went outside at the top that was enough for me. My legs were shaking all the way down the stairs. In fact I think they continued shaking until we got back to the camp.

On another occasion a top officer visited the camp and I have a photo of him when we paraded just outside the guard room.

(Later, in 1952, Sergeant Hillary, who was stationed at Plymouth, realised that I came from Hastings, and told me that his wife had given birth to a baby daughter in Fernbank, which was in Old London Road. He seemed to be quite a decent sort and had been awarded the Military Medal during the war. I went off with a Bombadier and another gunner to where some officers were having some sort of a refresher course for two weeks. We had to look after their kit etc. and also get their meals. It made a change but I must admit that it wasn't my cup of tea. Strangely as it happened, Sergeant Hillary was right there when we were unpacking our kit in the camp. He said to me, 'Oh, have you come back to do some more soldiering then Gunner Catt?'

I said, 'Well, I can't really stretch my imagination that far Sarge.')

Louie was still trying to get over his disappointment at having to do an extra six months. He thought that he would see if he could get home again on the next Wednesday afternoon. So, off he went and I thought that I would have a look to see who was who on battery orders. I was quite alarmed when I saw his name on there for guard on this night. He couldn't have looked at the orders but just took it for granted that he wasn't on. So I got up a plan of action. First of all I had a good clean-up of my best boots and then I changed and got ready for guard mounting at 5.50 to do a guard from 6.00. We mounted guard and then I saw the orderly officer striding towards us. Suddenly I realised that the orderly officer was the Regimental Sergeant Major. He checked us to make sure everything was in order and then when he got to me he said, "You're not Gunner Wonacott are you?"

"No sir, I am Gunner Catt, sir. I'm afraid Gunner Wonacott got taken ill a short time ago so I stepped into the breach sir. I'm sorry that I didn't have time to inform anyone sir, so I thought it would be best to hurry up and get ready to take his place."

"Yes, quite right Gunner Catt, that was very commendable of you."

I did the guard and in the morning I changed back to my second best uniform and boots. Later on in the morning when I saw my mate Louie I asked him if his mum and dad were alright. He said that they were and that they were pleased to see him again.

"Oh, that's good," I said. "By the way, have you looked up to see when you will be on duty?"

"No, but perhaps I'll do that as I have a feeling that I should be on duty soon."

So I went round with him to look at the orders and he suddenly said, "Oh dear, I should have been on guard last night. I shall be in trouble now."

"Don't worry, it's been taken care of, someone else did it in your place."

"What do you mean? Who would have done such a thing?" he said.

"I think he was a mate of yours who thought he would do you a favour."

He still seemed rather worried and said, "Who would have done such a thing and got himself in such a load of trouble?"

"Thanks for your confidence in me Louie, it's all been settled now. I did the guard and everything went off alright, even though it was the Regimental Sergeant Major who was on. I shouldn't think any more about it, if I was you. That's what mates are for."

"Well, you certainly are a mate doing something as important as that for me."

We did have a system when there were four of us on guard mounting. Of course only three of us did a guard, but the smartest one became what we called 'stick man' and he fell out without actually doing a guard. The idea was good but the trouble was that things descended into chaos. The main thing was the boots, which you could see your reflection in. This caused some jealousy and people went round slashing the toes of the boots, which you were unable to alter after that, so the idea was faded out. I must admit that I only got to be 'stick man' twice and in fact instead of going through this uproar it was easier to do a guard.

Louie's time for demob was getting closer. The night before he left I was on guard so I wasn't able to go out for a drink with them. However, I did say to him before they left, "I have something to say to you, because I feel I must before you go out. I don't want you to take offence but as you will be having a few drinks with the boys, instead of taking all your money with you, I'd like you to let me look after some of it for you, and I will keep it locked up in my locker".

"Of course I won't be offended, that's very thoughtful of you. I shall be sorry to say goodbye to you as I couldn't possibly have had a better mate."

In a way I was glad that I was on guard that night. The next morning there were bear hugs and all sorts of things going on and I thought that I would never meet a mate like that again. It really didn't feel the same without him. But now that Louie was demobbed I could think about my own demob getting nearer.

***

I had about six months to go and I got a posting to a survey unit on Salisbury Plain. I thought how daft is that: I had been at Plymouth for about 18 months and surely I would have been more use to them doing a job that I was trained for. What did I know about survey? You could have written my knowledge on the back of a bus ticket. So, a few days later I was off to Tilshead on Salisbury Plain. It was only a small camp, with four or five of us waiting on the officers.

It wasn't a bad job until after three days I disgraced myself. I committed an unpardonable crime. When I was serving the officers I hadn't noticed that there was a colonel at the dining table. He was the highest ranking officer at the table and of course he should have been served first. Because of this I was taken off waiting and put on stoking, which meant that I took it in turns to get the fires going at 5.30 in the morning. Also I heard another useful piece of information. The staff who were working at the camp were due for seven days' leave so I could put in for a week's leave. I had only a few weeks before I got demobbed and I didn't want to lose any leave. I wrote home to my mum and dad telling them that I would be coming home. I carried on lighting fires and keeping them stoked up. Two weeks later I went home on leave.

My mum and dad were pleased to see me for a whole week this time. We managed to get out and about and while I was there I said to them, "Don't forget I shall be home for good on Thursday July 19th."

I went back for a few weeks and finally left the camp and the Army for good. This time I had to get off the train at Eastbourne as I had to call in at a building called Goffs. This was where I had to hand in my army kit which I wouldn't need, and keep the kit which I would need for the Territorials. Then I was off home to Hastings, this time to settle down and no more going back after leaves.

45

Standing in the doorway of one of the billets. The chap wearing his best uniform was just going on guard. The one on his left got married a few weeks later and Les went to his wedding

Les's first day in the Army

Lined up outside the guard room waiting to be inspected by a
high-ranking officer at the School of Artillery

Chapter Five
Early Days in the
Parks Department

I thought that I would wait for a week or so before I started looking for work. It was quite amazing how many people, knowing that you were looking for work, would tell you about jobs that were so small and a long way away that it just wasn't worth entertaining them at all.

One job that I tackled in Harold Road had a back garden on rather a nasty slope. The only thing I could do was to make two small slopes about a third of the way down the garden and another slope the other two thirds of the way down the garden. We had 280 turfs delivered, to be carried down there, plus some sand and cement to make some steps with blocks.

I first of all made the two slopes and laid the turfs on them. Then I carried the rest of the turfs down and laid them on the more level parts of the lawn. After this there were just the steps to put down, which I had never tackled before. However, the old people who lived there seemed very pleased with it. The whole lot only cost £32 altogether. Of course this was July 1951, it would cost a bit more now.

I heard about a job at the top house in Linton Road, which I think was no. 30. Mr and Mrs Paskell lived there, but Mr Clark, who was Mrs Paskell's brother, owned the house. However he was hardly ever there as he always seemed to be going abroad somewhere. A gardener called Harry Penton worked at the house and he and his wife lived there. It was quite rare for Harry to work in the garden as he was always taking Mr Clark up to London Airport or bringing him home.

When Harry was out in the garden and we were working together I found that he was a very nice chap. He was interesting to talk to and also a good gardener.

I also got a job for a few weeks in St. Helens Avenue where I worked for an estate agent. It fitted in alright with one or two other jobs.

One day this estate agent came out when I was raking all the leaves and rubbish off the lawn and said, "Wouldn't you prefer to work in one place all the time instead of a day here and a day there? There is a lady who lives just down the road who is on the Parks Committee and she could put in a word for you to Mr Cassidy, the Parks Superintendent.'

"Well, that would be nice if it could happen," I replied. In just over a week I received a letter from the Parks asking me to call in and see Mr Cassidy on Monday week. When I got there he said there was a vacancy in an outside gang under Mr Held and I could make a start next Monday, February 18th 1952.

So this was marvellous. I knew Fred very well as he only lived just down the road from me. I got down to the park the following Monday and I saw Fred helping to load a box, some tools and a canvas shed onto a lorry. As I walked in the yard Fred called out, "Over here, Les!" So of course I went over to them and helped. Then Fred got into the cab with the driver and I got in the back of the lorry.

First of all, we all went up to the bottom of Churchill Avenue where another three chaps were waiting and we also loaded some tools on the lorry. We didn't go very far because our next job was just up the road near the top of Churchill Avenue. We unloaded all the tools from the lorry, plus the canvas shed which we put up. The next thing we had our 9.00 lunch. Our job after lunch was to plant some privet hedges in the gardens of some council houses so that people knew where their gardens finished.

We carried on to the top of Churchill Avenue to turf a bank and plant some trees and shrubs. This was right opposite the new school that was being built.

Fred then had a lot to say quietly as people walked by. We were able to hear what they were saying and Fred used to finish it off in his own words. Not loud enough for them to hear, but he was very good at that sort of thing. It certainly was quite amusing.

When we heard where we were going next we were very disappointed. It was out to the Firehills at Fairlight. I don't think that there could have been a colder place in Hastings at this time of year. The lorry came quite early, soon after 7.30, and picked up all our equipment and took us out there. We got all the tools unloaded, put up the shed and then it was time for lunch. We had to cut out some more fire lanes through the gorse and burn the rubbish. That was the warmest part of the job but of course you couldn't stay there for long. The lorry brought us back at about 4.30. We were out there for about a couple of weeks.

The next job was for three of us on the West Hill in Hastings. Fred and Harry were going to scythe the edges of the grass along the paths because in those days we didn't have mowers to do it. They would cut the edges, one each side and I would rake the grass down onto the path and then sweep it up. The barrow that I had to put it all in was quite massive. I think really it should have had a horse on it. I only needed a bag of oats to look the part. It was lucky that I was fairly tall.

To start with, I had to take it a long way, from the end of Collier Road or the Angel pub to the ladies parlour at the top of where the lift stopped. Gradually I didn't have to take it so far. The job lasted about a week altogether.

On Friday Fred asked me if I would pick up the litter on the West Hill the following day, Saturday, as

50

Jim, the chap who usually did it, was away on holiday. So I said that I would. It was a very easy job which made a change. Still, I couldn't really grumble as I had been working all over town in a short time.

On the next Monday we were drafted into the park called Coronation Wood. It was to clean up the rubbish and leaves, but it was an awful morning with drizzling rain. We soon realised that the weather wasn't going to improve so Fred, our charge-hand, said, "Come on, we'll get along to the park greenhouses, out of this."

We were only washing flower pots but we were in the dry and it was a job that had to be done anyway. While I was in there John Taylor, the deputy superintendent, arrived. He came over to me and said, "Oh Les, on Monday will you report to Warrior Square Gardens as you will be working there under Charlie Eldridge from now on."

I replied, "Oh that's good news as I'll be able to do some gardening then. Thank you, John."

I thought, at least I shall know where I shall be working each day from now on. That's what I thought at the time but of course it wasn't quite like that. So on the following Monday I set off for Warrior Square Gardens. There were about six gardeners and I actually knew one of them, Frank, who was two or three years older than me but he went to Ore Village School when I did during the war.

It seems that it was quite a nice little gang. I paired up with Taffy. His real name was George but the only reason he was called Taffy was because he came from Wales years ago.

To start off, we dug the borders on Warrior Square Gardens. After that we could be going anywhere along the Front Line which was three miles long, from the fish market to the bathing pool. Warrior Square was our depot.

One morning I was teamed up with Bernard. We went out to the fish market and he mowed the roundel in the middle of the road, while I just weeded and cleared up any rubbish and forked over the flower bed. Then Bernard said to me, "Would you take this bag of grass over to the lady in the pie shop?" The pie shop used to be on the corner of George Street and High Street.

When I handed this bag of grass over I said to the manageress, "Oh, I can see what you put in your pies now". She strongly denied it but it was no good!

Anyway, we got our tools together and went along to the town centre. Bernard was going to mow the lawns around the flower beds, of which there were five, while I trundled my hand mower across to the Memorial Clock Tower. After that I took my mower back across the road and I saw that there was a policeman standing next to the police box on the corner. As I reached him I said, "Could you tell me what the time is please?"

He looked at his watch and told me what the time was and then he said, "You've got a big clock over there." But strangely enough as the clock tower was about 30 feet high you couldn't see the time until you got away from it.

We got our mowers and tools together and moved a little way just around the corner where the sunken gardens were. There were two lawns here. All I could do was edging and clearing up in general. Then it was back to Warrior Square. On the way back there were seven small lawns to be mowed, but they would need to be done by hand mower. There was one by the pier, four in the middle and the other two were near the bottom of Warrior Square. I think Charlie, our foreman, must have read our thoughts because he suggested that Dave and I take the hand mowers out in the afternoon to mow those lawns. So off we went.

I went to the far one near the pier and left Dave in the middle where the four lawns were. By the time I got along to where Dave was the weather was looking decidedly dodgy. In fact it had actually started to rain and it looked stormy. We finished mowing those four lawns and then I said to Dave, "Come on, let's get down these steps into Bottle-Ally. I don't mind being the driver of the mower but I don't want to be the conductor as well."

So we made our way to the end of Bottle-Ally and the weather wasn't quite so bad so we nipped across the road and up to Warrior Square Gardens. By that time it was nearly home time.

The next morning Dave and I were sent out to the bathing pool which was the other end of the Front Line, just past West Marina Gardens. There were four lawns outside the bathing pool, two each side of the entrance to the pool itself. Then we had a few more lawns to mow on the way to Warrior Square. Also we mowed the two lawns which we had to leave from the afternoon before. So that cleared up the mowing. Except of course there were several big lawns which Frank used to mow with the big motor mower.

I remember one episode when the weather was so rough that it threw up a lot of the beach and those big lawns were absolutely covered. Four of us cleared all the stones off and sent them packing back to their rightful place.

The time had come to plant out the flower beds between the pier and Warrior Square Gardens. There were 12 flower beds; 10 long, narrow beds and two bigger beds which we called half-moon beds. They were spaced out between the longer beds.

One morning Harry and I had got our trolley loaded up overnight with 250 geraniums to plant in the first bed opposite Warrior Square. We came out and laid them out in four rows - two rows of 62 and two rows of 63. We managed to get them planted round about nine o'clock. Then we went back to our sheds in Warrior Square Gardens for our lunch. The next morning the other geraniums were sent out by tractor. We unloaded them and we had all the gang of six of us on that. We worked together very well, some of us laying them out and some following along planting them. By the end of the day we had most of the beds planted. The ones that we didn't have time to plant we took back in our truck to Warrior Square and brought them out the next morning to finish off.

That only left the two half-moon beds to plant. They would take longer because the beds were a lot bigger and would take a lot more plants. The plants used to be sent out from the nursery at Hollington. Charlie, our foreman, used to phone up from the phone box at the bottom of Warrior Square in case the weather was a bit dodgy. Then if the weather was alright they sent them out. The reason for this was that if the tide turned, it wasn't advisable to send them as if we had a lot of wind it was possible to lose the lot. Anyway, we were lucky with the weather and we managed to get the whole lot planted the same day.

Another problem was that if we didn't get any rain the plants had to be watered within two or three days to help them to get going. There were several stand pipes that we were able to use in that area.

The next borders to be planted were the large borders at West Marina, just past the Sun Lounge. I can't remember whether there were three of four along that end. Then there were the flower beds further along in West Marina Gardens or as the posh people called it, Grosvenor Gardens. In the gardens one man worked on his own, but when he wanted help we used to supply it. Once these gardens had all been planted we had finished. All that was needed now was weeding, hoeing and watering.

We used to have window boxes and baskets on the pier to keep watered as well. We usually did the watering every other day there, and I was often given the job.

One morning I went along soon after 7.30 to do the watering and I was almost knocked back in surprise when I lifted the trap door where the hose was, or should have been. Someone had kindly unscrewed the hose and thrown it all down on the beach. So I had to go down and carry it back up to the pier which wasn't very easy on my own, as it was quite heavy. I just hope that the person or persons had more fun than I did. When I got along to the shed in Warrior Square Gardens the other chaps were just coming out after having had their lunch. Charlie, the foreman, said, "What happened to you then, Les?"

I said, "Well, it looks as though someone had some fun and games as they helped me by undoing the hose which is under the bandstand floor and threw it down on the beach. I found it difficult to carry it back from the beach as it was quite heavy. When I got it all back I had to have five minutes rest."

"I should think so too, that was quite a job on your own. Anyway, we are going to West Marina Gardens, so will you come along there as well when you have had your lunch? Don't rush, but bring a trowel with you as some plants will be on the way now, hopefully."

By the time I got out there it would be almost 10 o'clock. Only a few of the flower beds were ready for planting so Charlie said, "Well, just plant the ones that are ready today and then after that two or three of you will have to come out here tomorrow and dig the other flower beds and get them ready for planting. Probably it will take the rest of the week to get the flower beds ready and early next week we'll get them to send the plants out from the nursery". It was nice to know that everything was coming along so well. I think that we had a good little gang who worked together well.

When the flower beds had been dug, I was the one who was picked to do the treading down before we planted them. I expect it was because I had the biggest feet. Still, we were often told to stand on our own two feet so I suppose that was why my feet were so big.

The only places left for us to plant out now were fairly small areas. There was the roundabout at the fish market and the two small flower beds in the centre of the road each side of the Albert Memorial Clock Tower. There were also five flower beds at Harold Place, above the toilets, and seven flower beds at Robertson Terrace. They are finished now but we always used to plant them out.

Other than that there were the sunken gardens. Rockeries led to the underground car park.

Charlie, our foreman, phoned up for them to bring the plants out first thing in the morning. One of our chaps went with the tractor and helped the driver unload one lot at the first port of call which was the fish market. He remained there and planted them and then they brought the other plants to the town centre and placed them where they were to be planted.

Robertson Terrace was a bigger area. We didn't plant all of them before we went to dinner at Warrior Square. In the afternoon we came back and finished the planting. I hadn't realised that there were still the flower beds on the lawn in Warrior Square Gardens. So the next day we planted them and finally that was that. Although all that planting was now done we still had the maintenance of them; namely weeding, hoeing and watering.

In 1953 I had to go on the Territorials two-week camp. We were taken there by lorry and when we arrived we had five-man tents to put up. Although the old gag says that the excitement was intense, believe me it wasn't. The first morning there was quite a shock as when we opened the tent flap the whole area was white with frost. Mind you, there was a bigger shock just round the corner. That was in the shape of a bowser which was being towed by an Army lorry which contained cold water for washing. All I could think of at that moment was that it was a good job this was only for two weeks. Of course in two weeks we may have had time to get used to it, but somehow I didn't think so.

When I got back to work the following Monday morning there were a few remarks passed about enjoying the holiday. I laughed it off and said, "Well, it was certainly different, we may go again next year".

They were now talking about making the lawn at the bottom of Warrior Square Gardens into a putting course. It was quite easy to take out the 18 holes once you had established where they were going. As none of us had ever done this before it was a new experience for us. For a start we went round and tried to place them in what we thought would be quite a good formation. Actually, we did change it a couple of times before we decided that it seemed about right. Now all we had to do was cut out the holes and put a metal pot into each hole.

I think at the time of opening the putting green it was only a shilling a round. It soon became popular, but of course when something new starts and a lot of people find that it's something they like, the price soon goes up. We found it quite difficult to cut the holes out at the start but it soon became easier.

More recently, I saw a couple of chaps cleaning up and painting the statue of Queen Victoria. I said to one of them, "Don't forget to put it back as it was, with a bullet hole in her right knee caused by a cannon shell during the war".

He said, " Yes, we've been told about that."

A job came about in the centre of Warrior Square Gardens, although not everybody agreed with it. Some of the flower beds were going to be filled and new flower beds made. Harry and I cut the turfs, loaded them onto our trolley and took them to the existing beds which were to be filled in. I said, "What do you want to do Harry, do you want to cut them, or roll them up and put them on the trolley?"

"Well I'll roll them up if you don't mind cutting them, Les?"

"No," I said, "I'm easy."

So away we went. I think that there were four flower beds to change round. They were about the same size so it worked out quite well. To be honest I really couldn't see the sense in it, but it wasn't for me to reason why, just to get on with it.

There were a couple of jobs involving alterations to the landscape along West Marina. Opposite the Victoria Hotel they were going to make a new flower bed on the sea side. The tractor arrived with some blocks which had to be laid and made into a new garden. Then the tractor brought a load of soil and Charlie and Harry made it nice and firm to bind the blocks together. Two or three of the other chaps threw the soil up onto a wheelbarrow. Guess who the barrow boy was? Yes, it was me. This job took about three days.

When it was finished there was another job to do about 30 yards away. A sunken garden was made. There was a big cactus bed in the middle and Bernard went and backed into it accidentally. He had to go home to get his wife to treat him. Unfortunately he lived at Hollington and came in on a bike. I often wonder whether he rode his bike home or whether he walked. I should have thought that it would have been better for him to have walked, it certainly would have been more comfortable. A little way away from here going towards the pier was the Sun Lounge. There were three flower beds between the footpath and the parade.

While we were trying to tidy these flower beds, I suddenly said to my mate: "I must get down to that crossing Harry or there will be an accident". So I jumped down quickly and I was just in time to stop a chap with a white stick step into the road. "What are you doing?" he said to me.

I said, "Well, you can't go across the road here."

He replied, "But I'm going across this crossing."

"Well, you could if there was one there. The crossing is a few yards away. What made you think that the crossing was just here?"

"Someone always brings me up the steps and puts me on the crossing."

"Well, that may be so but there are two flights of steps down to the Sun Lounge and it looks as though this person has come up the steps which are *not* opposite the crossing. If I were you I should make doubly sure another time."

After that we carried on with our job as though nothing had happened.

During the summer months we used to have a summer show on the White Rock Pavilion opposite the pier. It was on for several summers but I can't remember the years. Charlie asked me and Harry to prepare for the planting of a rose bed which ran along the bottom of the rose garden.

First of all there was a low wall along the bottom of the rose bed which would have to have the top knocked off it. As there was a greenhouse on the garden below this wall we had to lay some boards over the glass in case any of the debris came down. We did it one section at a time and then went down and moved the boards along further. Then we went back and knocked some more down. We carried on like this until the whole wall had been knocked down. The next day we covered the whole flower bed with manure. Then, a tractor-load of soil arrived at the nearest point to where we would be able to get at it with our wheelbarrow. There were just three steps to negotiate for the many barrows of soil. It took the rest of the day to clear all the soil from the steps. I don't know how many barrow loads there were but there must have been at least 30.

The next day we dug the rose bed and then planted the roses. The name of the rose was Masquerade, because this particular rose changed colour. Also the summer show which Cyril Fletcher and wife Betty Astell were in was called *Masquerade*.

They came to declare the flower bed open and there was quite a crowd of people there. Cyril Fletcher was very pleased. So a great day was had by all.

Les in 1951, after
leaving the Army

Aerial view of Warrior Square Gardens

The gang in 1952. Les was 21

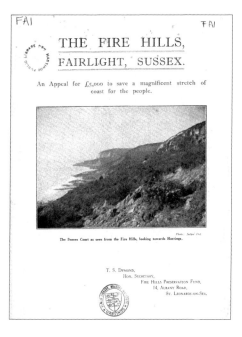

The Fire Hills,
Fairlight

Memorial Clock
Tower flower beds

63

The gang visited
Kew Gardens twice,
in 1952 and 1953

Digging a new flower bed opposite the Victoria Hotel

Geranium border

Masquerade rose

Linton Gardens today (this page and overleaf)

Chapter Six
Changes in the Town

By the 1970s the town and the area around it were changing fast. The Albert Memorial was taken down in November 1973. Harold Place had changed out of all recognition. The whole lot was removed and even the taxi rank which operated from the right side of the flower beds had to go, moving about 200 yards away to the bottom of Havelock Road.

The bus stop which was near the town centre, about where Kamsons the chemist is now, was closed to any buses. In fact the furthest that any traffic could go now was Wellington Square. A road was built over the top of an underground walkway. A new road was built from Wellington Square to the new seafront past where Woolworth's used to be.

In Pelham Street (which runs along the back of the new flats, built because the previous houses were bombed during the war), there used to be a nice little café called George's Café, where we would go for lunch when we were working in that area.

George was a very small man. However his wife made up for his lack of size as she was a very big lady. They also had a big boxer dog which used to sit just inside the door. He certainly used to look pretty vicious - not George, I mean the dog. I think he could be a handful if he was upset. Mind you, I don't think anyone ever tried it.

Also there used to be a café right on the seafront called The Criterion which was next to the pub. Just along from there right in the middle of the road there was a big rockery. One day a tractor came in and told us that he had orders to remove the rockery. It took three of us and the tractor driver three or four days to clear it away. It was very hard work as there were several quite hefty rocks there.

The next thing to go was the glass shelter where people used to sit reading, or perhaps sleeping. There was enough room for about 10 or 12. The only shelters there now are the ones overlooking the sunken gardens. I used to think that the people were watching me work, but after a while I just didn't take any notice as I got used to it.

Sometimes when the putting green was open in Warrior Square and there wasn't a regular attendant we used to take it in turns to do one evening on the green. This consisted of four hours. We didn't get paid any extra money but instead we had the time off. We left at 11.30 in the morning.

I remember that George (Taffy) and I were working alone on the sunken gardens one morning. When I said that I was going home soon George said, "Oh, how will I be able to tell what the time is? I shall be here on my own."

"Well you can look at a watch to tell the time, George," I replied.

"That's the thing Les, I haven't got a watch."

"That's alright, you can have a look at mine. I'll let you have it until tomorrow."

"Would you really trust me with your watch until tomorrow?"

"Well, of course I would, after all it's only a pocket watch."

"What about if I drop it or something?"

"Oh, you won't do that and if you did I know you would buy me another one. So if I'm not worried, why should you be? As I say, I know if anything like that happened I know you would be very happy to buy me a new one."

When I walked into the shed at Warrior Square in the morning he hurried out to meet me with my watch. "Oh thanks George," I said, "I did feel quite lonely without it."

Then the rest of the gang took it up and said, "Do you mean to say you loaned him your watch, Les? That was a risky thing to do."

"Of course I relied on him, he is a work mate after all. I'd trust him with my watch, the same as I would trust any one of you."

They were quiet after that when they realised that I would have trusted any of them.

Charlie told us that starting next week a gang were coming into Warrior Square Gardens to re-tarmac the paths. "Taffy and Les, you will be cutting back on the edges of the lawn and rolling the turf back, and when they have finished you can put the turf back again," said Charlie.

So we set about doing that and it was quite a big job. First of all we marked it out. Then we started to roll the turfs back so that when they had finished we would be able to relay the turf. Of course we had to have a good start on them and roll up quite a lot of the turf so that we could get a good way in front. This was the centre part of the gardens that they were tarmacing.

We found that we also needed some soil as the height of the new tarmac was two or three inches higher. When we re-laid the turf it would have to be that much higher than the paths.

It wouldn't seem much higher but with the area that we would have to cover it was still a lot of work. Anyway, we moved ahead in rolling the turfs back out of their way. There were about four in the tarmac gang so we had to get some way ahead because otherwise they would soon have caught up with us. It worked out pretty well. It wouldn't matter how far ahead we got as we could always drop back and relay the turf. It took most of the week as it's surprising how much work it made. It was a job that needed to be done and I think everyone was pleased with it.

I remember the plants that were sent from Wishing Tree Nursery. When some of us first worked up there, there weren't any greenhouses, just the laying out ground for plants like wall flowers and polyanthus. The only form of cover we had at that time was a couple of sheds which were made of metal and were open at both ends. We could manage to sit in there to have our lunch or dinner but that was about all. It was a lot different later on when they started to build the greenhouses. I didn't know at that time that I was going to be working up there for about 18 months.

In the autumn, George and I had to go out to West Marina Gardens to dig the big border. It was on the sea side of the gardens, about 50 or 60 yards long. On the day we were out, a bitter cold wind was blowing. It was a good job there was a tall hedge that helped to keep the wind off. As we were digging away we had a visitor in the shape of the Deputy Superintendent. He came over and spoke to us and said what a nice morning it was.

"Yes, but it's a cold wind," said George to him.

"Yes, but it's very bracing," he replied.

If it was so bracing I don't know why he was so eager to get away. Anyway, we were very thankful for that tall hedge to keep some of the wind out. We had to go back to digging the border the next day, Friday, and Charlie said that he wanted two of us to help the chap with the bowling green on Monday. This chap worked on his own all the year round. However when any big jobs cropped up we had to supply help from the Front Line staff. On Monday the sand was being delivered to dress the bowling green, and it really needed three of us.

We got out there about 8.00 in the morning and the sand had just been delivered as near the bowling green as possible. So first of all we carried the planks across the green and laid them from corner to corner because that was the most direct route. Then I got into my place as the barrow boy. When we first started I couldn't keep up with them. I just tipped the sand onto the green and made my way back to get the next load. While I was gone they had to alter the runway of boards each time. After a while my trip was getting shorter whereas they were still having to move the boards. As I had more time between loads I started to help them by moving the boards as well. It really was quite a job but I was glad of the experience.

The next day we both went back to West Marina Gardens to carry on with digging that large border. The man who was working in the gardens all the time used to spend an hour, or perhaps an hour and a half, raking the bowling green so that the sand was gradually worked into the green. Before we put the sand on as a dressing we had made holes all over it. Therefore, by continually using a special rake it gradually worked into the green.

One afternoon we went along to Marina after we had finished working in West Marina Gardens and started cleaning up the rockeries. There were three of us with our three-wheeled truck. There was a lot of rubbish and we had to leave about 4.00 to get ourselves and our rubbish back to Warrior Square Gardens by 4.30. We were going past the church which had been newly rebuilt as it had been bombed during the war. We had our rubbish and all our tools on our truck when a bus pulled up at the stop near St. Leonard's Church. There was a conductor standing on the platform of the bus. As I was on the front of the truck I called out to the bus conductor, "Hang on, we want this bus!"

He looked at us in horror and exclaimed, "You can't get on my bus with all that lot!"

The next day we cleared all the rubbish out of a flower bed called Undercliffe which was in the shape of a half moon. As it wasn't a very big bed we brought the plants along in our truck and planted it out as well. The whole Front Line had been planted now. All we needed to do was to keep it weeded, hoed and watered. We were a bit thwarted by a spell of wet weather when we weren't able to work on the beds. It was dreary just messing about in the sheds, cleaning up tools etc. Of course we were bound to get some wet days. The only good thing was it stopped us from having to water the flower beds.

The whole Front Line has altered now, with all the changes that have been made. The rockery in Warrior Square Gardens was in need of attention so two or three of us had a go at that. There was a man who was staying at one of the hotels in Warrior Square who used to prowl around the rockeries looking for snails. I think he used to take them back to his hotel and eat them.

As I pointed out earlier if the Department hadn't got enough staff to do jobs in one particular garden they would often send out for help. On one particular morning they needed help at Gensing Gardens which is about half way up London Road. The staff at Gensing Gardens was only three and they sent down to Warrior Square for some help. Apparently they didn't have enough people to dig a big border that stretched down into London Road. There was only one chap they could spare from Gensing Gardens itself so they needed a couple of us to go up there to help out. The trouble too with this border was that there were trees and shrubs growing in it. I thought to myself, this will be awkward for the person digging in the middle. I wasn't left to wonder who that would be for long. It seemed that it was going to be me.

We started off alright until my mate who came up

with me from Warrior Square Gardens got quite het up because he thought that he was doing more digging than the two of us.

He suddenly let fly by saying, "It's all very well isn't it but I'm digging half of the border myself while you two are digging the other half. So I am doing twice as much work."

I tried to explain to him that sometimes I had to dig on one side to go round a shrub and another time I had to go round the other side. I couldn't make him see that he wasn't doing any more work than anyone else. I didn't like what he was implying. Never in my years of gardening have I let anyone do my share of the work. In fact, sometimes I have done more than my share and I've been pleased to do so.

I'm afraid that this conversation has stayed with me all my working life.

There are several other gardens where I worked during my time on the Parks and Gardens, including Linton Gardens and St Leonard's Gardens.

St Leonard's Gardens in Maze Hill was a very nice garden to work in. They were called 'blind' gardens as there was a blind home near there. In fact I think that it is still there. In St Leonard's Gardens most of the plants had a distinct smell to them so that any blind people going in the gardens would be able to tell what flowers they were by their smell. What a nice thought.

I have also worked in Alexandra Park on numerous occasions. Years ago there used to be a small nursery for growing plants. Then of course we used to go out to various gardens in the town. A lot of them used to get planted in the park itself.

It was all very well to keep going all over the place like this but one day I felt that whenever they wanted anyone to help someone else out that my name seemed to be the one to come out. I found that it was very difficult to get interested in the work you were doing when you got moved on to somewhere else.

So one day I made up my mind and just walked into The Parks office in Alexandra Park and gave in my notice. I had never been known to make rash decisions but I thought afterwards that maybe I had made one now. Anyway, it was my decision and if anything went wrong I only had myself to blame.

When I saw the different chaps in the park during the time I was working my notice they couldn't believe it. In fact several of them asked me if it was true. I began to wonder if it was true myself. Anyway, I walked out of the park on the Friday night with quite mixed feelings. My mum and dad didn't try to talk me out of it because they knew once my mind was made up there wouldn't be anything that would shift my resolve.

Chapter 7
Private Gardening

I had already written out several cards to put into newsagents and shops around the town. Towards the end of the week I had received several replies and one of my first jobs was to get in touch with these people. One that looked promising was a nursing home on the corner of Old Roar Road and another was on Tower Road West.

The one at Oaklands Nursing Home I answered by letter and suggested calling in to see them at the end of that week. I also made an appointment to look at Tower Road West. The only fly in the ointment with the nursing home was that it was for five days a week from 7.15 to 12.15. So if they had no objections I would go to Tower Road West on Saturday mornings for five hours each week. That would be the start anyway. Any other jobs that I heard about I would have to fit in, in the afternoons.

There was bound to be a bit of a scramble to start with but I was sure things would work out alright. The people who lived at Tower Road West had quite a big garden and I suggested five hours from 8.00 to 1.00 on Saturdays and we seemed to have a plan there. They had one little girl, about six years old.

The next week I started looking for another five afternoons' work. I began work for a builder in Wykeham Road, near Braybrook Road, and soon after that the couple who lived opposite wanted me to go there one afternoon a week. By now I only had one afternoon when I needed work. I was pretty sure that something would soon turn up.

It was surprising but a number of people told me about jobs that were practically non-existent. For instance, they would tell me about a small job that would have taken longer to get there and back than it would to do the whole job. So when I asked them whether it was worthwhile to do this job they were slightly resentful.

I managed to keep going but I must admit it wasn't the piece of cake that I thought it would be. On the other hand there were plenty of gardens around that you could see hadn't been gardened for years.

One job that I took on was at Collier Road, not far from Priory Road School, where I finished my schooling. I had only worked there for a short time when they told me that they were going on holiday the following week and that they would pay me two weeks' money when they came back. There was also a painter working indoors. They had a little black and white cat and I wondered how he was going to manage. When I went there the following week I walked along to the end of Priory Road where they had an off license and bought a pint of milk and a tin of cat food. When I got back I saw that the painter was still working there and he had also gone shopping for the cat. Still, I didn't mind, as I felt that it was worth it.

I also took on a gardening job in Godwin Road and when I had been there for a few months the people next door to them asked me to look after their garden too. That is a bit dodgy really when you work for neighbours like that, but as both families were good friends it worked out alright.

The one that I went to first had a big Siamese cat who was very friendly. One morning I was having my lunch in the porch at the back and when the lady came out with a cup of tea he was curled up on my lap. She was very surprised and said, "Well, I've never known him to get on anyone's lap before".

So I replied, "Well, perhaps he realises that I am also a cat, even though it's only in name".

At the nursing home where I worked the old chap came over to me one day and said, "Whatever you do don't go over there where those leaves are as I've got an idea there is a wasp nest there". So I thanked him for telling me and I carried on working.

Suddenly, all hell seemed to break loose as the old chap was yelling like someone who had gone mad. He was tearing across the lawn with a stream of wasps following him. I couldn't understand why he had taken the trouble to come over and tell me about the wasps and then go over poking about himself. I really felt quite sorry for him even though he was a grumpy old man.

Sometimes, when I had done a job in the garden and he didn't like it he would criticise it. So I didn't see him for the rest of the day. I expect his wife who was the matron was still treating his wounds.

I used to go up to the French windows when they rang the bell at about ten o'clock and collect my cup of tea and bring it down to the shed and then return the empty cup. One particular day I was up at the top of an apple tree, pruning, when the bell rang. Naturally enough, it took me several minutes to collect my cup of tea. They didn't seem to notice that but when I took the empty cup back the old chap accused me of taking such a long time having my lunch. I soon answered him by saying, actually I hadn't had any longer for my lunch, the truth was if anything I've probably had less time as when the bell went I was up the top of an apple tree which took me some time to get down.

In another way I was sorry to leave working with the Front Line gang. That was because I had met and made friends with a very remarkable man. He was the putting attendant at Warrior Square Gardens. His invitation to me to go to see the wrestling on his television set was a very wonderful thing for me, more than he ever realised. Also he always listened to other people's troubles even though he was a very sick man himself, but he made no bones about his own health. Anyway, I'm afraid he had to go into the hospital and I was able to visit him a couple of times. Then one evening when I went to the hospital to see him I had to enquire where he was and they told me the very sad news that he had died.

I caught a bus to the old town to see his wife and daughter, Emily, and I spent the rest of the evening with them. Of course I went to his funeral. After the funeral I still used to go to his house some evenings, but not just to see the television, but also to see Emily. A little while later I plucked up my courage and asked Emily if she would go out with me one evening. The very first date we went on was to the De La Warr Pavilion at Bexhill to see wrestling. It was a very nice evening, especially the company.

After that we used to go out for walks sometimes. One particular walk we went on I asked Emily if we could get engaged. She was quite surprised but she said that she would give me the answer the next time we met. So I was on thorns for three days until we met up again. I was very pleased with the answer because we agreed to get engaged.

One of the next things I needed to do was call in at the jeweller's and buy an engagement ring. When I went to work after the weekend, one or two people asked me if I had seen the World Cup match on television. I said no, I was doing something much more important. One of the chaps said, "How could anything be better than watching England win the World Cup?"

I replied, "But I did, I bought an engagement ring". They just gasped as they had no idea what I was planning.

Soon after that when Emily and I were out walking I said that we should look for a house to buy. She was surprised but as we were both in our thirties I thought that it ought to be soon.

So we got married on January 14th 1967 and we had a very nice time. The vicar was a very short man and he had to stand on a box. We held the reception at Eversfield Place Hotel. Monica, a friend of Emily's for a good few years, and her husband came. Also, their two young daughters were our bridesmaids. I think they were five and six years old at that time. While we were at the reception the youngest daughter Fiona said, "Does that mean we have to come and live with you now?"

"No, that wouldn't do and I don't think your mum would be too pleased, do you?"

Emily's Uncle Charlie gave her away but of course we all wished that it had been Emily's dad. I wished it had been possible for him to have been my father-in-law, but it wasn't to be.

We went house hunting with various estate agents. Then one day we walked into a house in Harold Road and directly we walked into the kitchen we both thought 'this is the one'. It was reasonably priced and if we put a good amount of cash down we should be able to get a reasonable amount to pay each month on the repayments over 20 years. We had taken the opportunity of buying the bare essentials for the time being. Then, when we had got enough money we gradually bought the rest of the furniture.

The gardens were in a bit of a mess but that was my forté. It looked as if someone had thrown their rubbish in what would be our back garden.

As I say the house was in quite good order. One of the main things to be done was to replace the stair carpet which was a bit grotty. So one weekend I spent all day Saturday taking the old carpet up. I'm afraid Emily had the worst job of all in having to clean the stairs down, 17 of them. Then I laid the new stair carpet. First of all I had to put a steel grip screwed into each stair. Then I measured each stair from the straight wall which was between our house and next door – 27″. Then I let all the carpet out and gradually worked my way down the stairs. We lived in that house for 47 years and the carpet was almost as good as when it was new. The only ones which needed replacing were the bottom two stairs.

The next thing was some of the electrics were a bit dodgy so it was important to get them done.

Not long after these jobs were done, we felt that we would like to have a retaining wall built at the back. But there was rubbish everywhere. There was a bank which had trees and shrubs on it. So, first of all, I spent about two hours each evening clearing all the rubbish from the front garden. That took a couple of evenings. Then I started to cut down the trees and shrubs and pile them up in the front garden. Then I turned to the rest of the rubbish which I carried through from the back. I had to dig out this bank of soil and carry the soil through to the front garden in a bucket. After about three or four weeks you could hardly see the front garden at all. So I ordered one of the big buckets to be brought for me to fill up. When it arrived I spent Sunday mornings throwing the branches, etc. into the bucket. After that I spent at least two hours throwing all the soil in there every evening.

Then I had a week's grace when I didn't do any more evening work. But I had been in touch with a builder who we arranged to come and build the wall for us. So the following week I made an arrangement for a yard of ballast and some bags of cement to be delivered. Also 100 blocks for the wall. When I got home from work about five o'clock there was all this ballast tipped in the road. Also 100 blocks were stacked on the pavement up against the wall. So, first of all I carried some of the blocks up the steps and laid them halfway across the steps so that we would have half of the width of the steps to get in and out of the front door. Then I started to throw this ballast on the inside of the blocks. It was quite a job and altogether it took me about four hours. After that I spent the next two evenings carrying all the ballast through to the back and also the blocks. I spent three hours each evening for two evenings to finish getting it all out the back ready for the bricklayer who was coming the following week. I had a couple of free evenings after this.

The next week I would be on a week's holiday so I would be able to help the bricklayer. I got the blocks to him and mixed up the cement. The only thing I didn't do was to actually build the wall. I realise of course that's a special skilled job. But he finished the wall in about three days and I was thankful to have a bit of rest after that. However, by helping like I did, it cut the cost by about half.

I found that I was getting plenty of gardening jobs now and a lot of information seemed to come through a friend of a friend. Very often I found that I was working in gardens which were either next door to one another or very close. The cry was, "Oh you can come and tidy our garden next". On one occasion I was going to three houses in Moscow Road in Clive Vale and also four houses together in Canute Road near Christ Church, Ore. Of course it was a bit tricky working in such close proximity as you had to make sure that you didn't neglect any of them and spend too much time making the others better. I think a bit of jealousy used to go on. Anyway, it seemed to work out pretty well.

Eventually I got rather fed up with working at Oaklands Nursing Home and I wasn't really enamoured with the idea of starting there at 7.15 in the morning. My usual time of starting was 8.00 which

I think was early enough. Also the old chap was very cantankerous. There wasn't a thing that I did right in the garden for him and I wasn't prepared to put up with that. Near to where he lived there was an old lady at 243, Sedlescombe Road North who I was told needed a gardener. So I went to see her and she needed someone for about half a day a week. So I told her my terms and that I could make a start in about two weeks' time. She seemed to be very pleased. So the next time I went to the nursing home I gave in my notice. The old chap was livid that I was going to be leaving. He really went up in the air. Not that I took any notice of that as he only had to come down again.

Oddly enough, when I started work for the old lady she told me that her sister had spoken about someone who lived just along the road at No. 480 who needed a gardener for a couple of days a week.

First of all I thought that I would make sure that I get the motor mower out to tidy the lawn. Mind you, I thought that I had bitten off more than I could chew because the mower was one that I wasn't conversant with. Anyway, the man from next door helped me to get the mower going. I say he helped me, but I don't think that I had much to do with it really.

I managed to get the lawn mowed and did one or two other jobs as well and told her that I would go along to No. 480 next week. The new house was called Roselands and the owners were Mr and Mrs Gaze. I could see why the house was called Roselands. There was a long drive from the road down to their gate of about 100 yards. Also there was a four-foot-high fence all the way down the drive which was absolutely covered in rambler roses. It must have been a picture when they were all in flower. I said that I would make a start the following week but only for half a day for two weeks. Then after that I would come for two days a week. They seemed to be quite pleased with that.

So I made a start the following week, but of course it was such a big garden it was a bit of a problem to know where to begin. However, after I had a look around the garden I got some idea where the worst places were. They had a big back garden and even after I had tidied it, it would still require me to do the two days to keep it tidy.

They had several fruit trees which would need to be pruned before 21st March, the first day of spring, though that was some time away yet.

One question Mr Gaze did ask me was with such a long drive would I be willing to go up there to dig them out if we had a lot of snow: "Otherwise we shall be cut off." I assured him that I would.

That winter we had a big fall of snow. It was the most snow I could ever remember at one time. I cleared our front steps and footpath about 8.00 in the morning. Then I cleared the snow from our back yard so that we would be able to get to our outside toilet.

Then I said to my mum that I could hear a cat crying somewhere. I cleared the snow from our back steps up to the back garden and I saw this black and white cat crouched right up into the corner of the garden. His coat was all white and it looked frozen. So I picked him up and knocked all the ice from his coat. It was amazing that he was still alive. As I got him down from the garden the old lady who lived three doors away and had five cats came towards me, swimming through the snow, and took her cat from me and went indoors with him.

I said to my mum, "Could we have our dinner a bit early so that I can get up to the Ridge". She agreed and we had dinner about 12.00. I started walking but it was very slow going as the snow was over the top of my Wellingtons. As I walked up round the ridge there was a Corporation snow plough trying to clear one half of the width of the road. Opposite Pine Avenue where there was a bus stop and a hedge there was so much snow that it was completely covered.

I gradually made a bit of progress and by the time I got to Roselands the time was about 1.45. The snow was about four feet deep because it was up to the top of the fence. As I stood looking at it, wondering what to do, a chap came out of one of the houses opposite with a spade and said, "I think you'll need this". How right he was. It took me until four o'clock just to get a little nick in the snow down to the gate. Mr Gaze looked out his front door and said, "Is there much snow Les?"

"Yes, there is quite a lot, in fact it is level with the top of the fence so that means that it is about four feet deep. Anyway, I shall be walking home now and I'll see you in the morning although it won't be very early as I shall have to walk. In fact I don't think there will be any buses up here for a while."

So I took the spade back to its owner and started the walk home. I think that I arrived about 6.00. I must admit that I really was dog tired - although my name is Catt. In fact I can honestly say that I had never been so tired in all my life.

Whatever happened the next day I felt that it couldn't be as bad as today. So I set out walking just before 8.00 in the morning and got to Roselands about 9.30. I managed to get down to the shed and pick up a spade. By the time I got back up to the top of the drive it was about 10.00 and I saw the cleaning lady struggling through the snow. I tried to help her by going down the drive, making the little niche which I had started the day before a little bit bigger. It took the both of us about another half an hour to get down to the front gate. As I left her at the door I said to her that I would help her up to the top of the drive when she finished work. So by the time she went I had been able to make things a little better. This was the only way to go about things really as there was so much snow to move. It took most of the week really before I started to feel that I was getting anywhere. I went on the Saturday but I admit that I didn't go on Sunday. I actually had only one day away from it all. I really was glad of a day's rest.

On Monday morning I left home just before eight o'clock to start walking again and got to work just after nine o'clock. I helped the lady cleaner down to the house and then I carried on clearing the snow. I was digging snow and throwing it over into the field. One day when I was clearing the snow we had a blizzard and all the snow that I cleared that day blew back and I had done a day's work without anything to show for it. Altogether I spent perhaps a couple of weeks before the snow started to melt away.

Mr Gaze said to me, "Well you've done a great job clearing that lot Les, but as there isn't anything that can be done in the garden there are several jobs that need doing in the garage. There are some steps and a ladder that need painting".

So at least I had quite a bit of work to do inside. I was glad that a lot of the snow was going away now and I was beginning to be able to do one or two little jobs outside. Of course I wasn't sure when the buses would start to run but it could be soon. As I say I was beginning to get one or two little areas tidied up now.

I must admit that I didn't foresee the exceptionally bad weather coming. Maybe we were out of the woods now, I thought. It certainly made you realise how dodgy gardening was. I think most people are not aware of the pitfalls. They are what I would call 'fair weather gardeners'. They just go into the garden when the sun shines and they don't seem to realise that gardening isn't always for fine days.

The snow had given me quite a jolt. I was giving a lot of thought as to how wise I had been to leave the

Parks Department where you were able to work regardless of the weather.

With this in mind on the following Monday I made my way to the Superintendent's office in the park and asked if there were any vacancies. I was told that there was a vacancy at White Rock Gardens and I could make a start on the following Monday.

So then I made my way up to Roselands with a heavy heart. When I got up there and rang the bell I told them that I had some very bad news for them. I said that because of the very bad weather this morning I went over to Alexandra Park to see if there were any vacancies and the result was that I should be starting back on the Parks and Gardens at White Rock Gardens next Monday. I was very sorry to have to leave them in the lurch like this but I really couldn't afford to take a chance about the weather again.

I had been away from the Parks and Gardens for three years and I think I had learnt a few lessons. Not all of them good, I must admit. With one week to go I did feel that I would like to put myself out at Roselands and do that little bit extra and get things as tidy as possible before I left. Although I shouldn't really have felt like that. After all, look how I had worked clearing all that snow. That was really hard. In fact all that walking through the deep snow, I wonder who else would have done that.

Emily arrives with her Uncle Charlie on her and Les's wedding day,
January 14th, 1967. Uncle Charlie gave her away

More pictures of Les and Emily's wedding

Emily's parents
Henry Betts, after
WW1
Emily Dann, aged
17-18, in WRAF
uniform, in WW1

Chapter Eight
Return to the Parks

On the Monday morning just before 7.30 I arrived at the mess room at White Rock Garden. I said a cheery "Good morning everybody," because some I knew their names and some I didn't. Most of them gave me an answer. As the weather had been so bad in early 1963, everyone was behind with their gardening work. The work that should have been done earlier in the year hadn't been started. A gang of about half a dozen of us went up to the sunken gardens which is near to the Oval and the football pitch. There was a mountain of leaves to rake up. We put them all in a pile for the tractor to pick up.

One of the chaps did say something about going to the boss with cap in hand. I realised that he was alluding to me but I didn't reply to the innuendo because I felt that it wasn't worth it as I hadn't done anybody any harm. So I just carried on clearing up the leaves and kept my head down as I felt that I wasn't responsible for how they felt. If I had done anybody out of a job it would have been different.

We had a good load of leaves in a pile ready for the tractor to pick up in the afternoon. He took it to the tip while the rest of use made our way back to White Rock Gardens. I'd picked my seat in the corner of the mess room and waited to see if anyone else was going to claim it but they didn't. I began to be part of the gang and I didn't have a preference at all for what job I was given, so there wasn't anyone that could fault me there. We had some snow shortly after, but it was nothing like the amount we had on New Year's Day. It was enough to cover the paths in the gardens so we split up into two small gangs and got the paths clear between us. Then we had to go outside and get the snow off the public footpaths. I have a photo of us clearing snow just above the Oval football pitch. There were several of us on this job and as you can see Paul Joy is one of them. I knew he came from a fishing family but he worked on the Parks and Gardens for several years before he went back to fishing. One morning I saw his dad walking down the Bourne and I said to him, "What, are you going off fishing then Mr. Joy?"

He replied, "What, me, at my age? I'm 94."

"Oh, so you're not going then?" I said.

Soon after I had started back at White Rock Gardens a hover mower was delivered which stood in our mess room. Everybody seemed to be admiring it and wondering who was going to have the privilege of using it. I just kept out of it as I thought that we would know soon enough. We weren't left wondering for very long because our foreman said to me, "Les, will you bring the new mower which will be used for mowing the banks". I followed him over to the other side of Falaise Road and made a start on the easier bank, opposite the putting office.

The trouble with this mover was that after the grass had been cut on the bank someone had to rake it all up. There were three or four banks in that area. The next one was quite big, running from just below the tennis courts along to the tennis pavilion. Also it went right up to The Oval football pitch.

As this was the first time these banks of grass had been cut there was plenty of grass to collect up. That wasn't too bad but the next one was a lot worse. It went right round the top of The Oval which was quite steep. Then I mowed the lower bank which ran along Cambridge Road. It was a smaller bank but it was surprising when I came to rake it up how much grass there was there. I was very pleased when this job was completed because the whole area of grass had been cut so it was nice and smart for the weekend.

I had been warned by our foreman that the next week the rest of the banks in the gardens were to be cut. So I started on the bank below the bowling green except that there was a match on. The problem was that as it was so dry a lot of dust blew up. I did apologise that I hadn't been aware of the match but said I would talk to my foreman and ask him to leave it to a time when there wasn't a match on.

When I spoke to Fred about it he said it would be best to leave it for now and to come back at another time. So the next week, on a day when there wasn't a match, I was asked to mow it and afterwards we raked it all up and took it away. I must say it did look a treat when it had been done, but of course it's not for me to say.

The worst banks to mow were the ones in Bohemia Road but when they were done that was the lot. I was very thankful when they were all finished, as the weather was so hot the sweat used to run off me. In fact although I got home about 5.00 I couldn't have my dinner until about 6.00 when I had finally stopped sweating.

It was nice that it was done for now but of course it would soon want mowing again, probably in about two or three weeks' time.

I used to mow the putting green every week. I would try and mow it on Mondays as the ladies had a club which played every Tuesday afternoon and I wanted it to be playable for them. It would seem that I was being consigned to looking after that side of the gardens with the help of a mate. Of course several people were needed when there was planting to be done. As is the way of things, everything seemed to need doing at the same time. However we did gradually get it done.

Two of us used to work on the other side of Falaise Road. That was known as the games area. There were 17 tennis courts and a putting green. One morning Frank, the foreman, got me, my mate Harold. and Paul Joy to go up to the Oval and dig out some shrubs. This was on the Oval football pitch in Bohemia Road. There were about 20 shrubs, all growing alongside the wall of the school. So, we started digging away. I don't know why but most people seem to have the misconception that if they dig out a small amount of soil that the object will just jump out of the ground. Nothing is further from the truth. I had dug quite a lot of soil out and actually gone underneath the shrub when Paul said to me, "I can see that you have done this job before, Les."

"Yes, I have a few times, Paul, it's like everything in life, it's never as straightforward as you think it's going to be," I replied.

I know that my next-door neighbour in Harold Road was digging about near the wall which separates our gardens. I was rather interested know what he was doing so I had a look over there. I said, "Hello Dave, how's it going?"

"Alright Les, I'm having a bit of a job with this shrub." When I looked there was a small shrub and he had got about two inches of soil out.

"Would you mind if I gave some advice on how to make it easier Dave?" I asked.

"Not at all," he replied.

"Well, first of all take out quite a lot of soil so that you can get underneath the shrub and it will just pull out of the ground." With this in mind, he found it easy to finish the job.

One morning as I walked through White Rock Gardens, as I passed No. 1 Tennis Court, there were two men playing tennis. The ball kept hitting the top of the net. So I strolled in there and let the net down and said, "You're not hitting the ball properly, it keeps hitting the top of the net". They both started to shout at me, and I said, "Never mind, it wasn't too bad," and we all three laughed.

While I was working at White Rock Gardens I found myself in excruciating pain in my back, hardly able to walk. I called in at Hollingsworth's, the car dealers in Braybrook Road, where my wife worked. I was driven home by one of the directors, I think by one of the sons. Within a couple of days I was picked up by an ambulance and taken into the East Sussex Hospital in Cambridge Road. I was put into traction with both legs. I don't know why they called it traction as it was no 'attraction' to me.

I didn't realise that I was going to have to stay in hospital for 22 days. After about 18 days a woman physiotherapist came to help me with some exercises. A couple of days later she said to me, "Can you walk round the ward yet?" I said with some surprise that I could hardly walk around the bed. After a couple of weeks I left hospital and was able to go back to work.

As well as the various gardens there was a lot of work needed to be done where they were building council houses. I worked on one of them in Broomsgrove Road. Also there was Blackman Avenue and Wishing Tree Road in Hollington. It consisted of moving a lot of soil around and laying lawns.

When the weather was bad, such as a lot of rain, we were drafted into the Wishing Tree Nursery as there was always plenty of work there. This consisted mainly of potting up geranium cuttings and sorting out the bulbs for the next year. I worked up there for about 18 months at one time.

One day when I was working on the council estate I got drafted up to the Grammar School ground in St. Helens Road. This job was quite foreign to me as they were relaying a cricket wicket. This is a very accurate way of laying turf. You needed two things - a good eye and an incredible amount of patience.

At the start you had to take up a couple of rows of turf and move them over to the other side of the running track. This was to give you room to make a start on the third row of turf. So, as you used your turfing iron to take up the turf from the third row you turned around and laid the turf on the first row. You had quite a number of pegs which you had to lay the turf to and a board to ensure that it was dead level. This had to be done with every turf that you laid.

As you can imagine this required an enormous amount of patience as when you first started you didn't seem to be getting anywhere. There were three or four of us in a line but it took at least a couple of days to get the hang of it. But something was destined to change things on the second day.

George, the charge hand who was with us, came over at almost the end of the day and quite meekly announced that he couldn't find his keys. So we knew what this meant. We started taking up most of the turf which we had taken two days to lay. We didn't feel very pleased because we had done all that work for nothing.

There was another shock when George walked out of the pavilion and said in a meek little voice, "I've found my keys in the pavilion". We all seemed to hold our breath. That was at least two days work we had lost. It was a good job that we were good-tempered otherwise we might have lynched him. Once we got our breath back we carried on for another three days until we finished the work. I just hoped that I wouldn't get any more jobs like that. Since then I have laid turf in several places and for various sports.

***

A True and Poignant Tale of Two Cats

When we lived in Harold Road a ginger cat started coming across our back garden. He was very thin. He used to turn up every day and although we felt very sorry for him we didn't want to start feeding him as we had a cat of our own. This went on for about six weeks and although we made enquires round about, none of our neighbours seemed to know anything about him.

I got in touch with the animal protection society and they said that they would come and pick him up at about 11.00 the next morning. When the lady turned up I went up to the back garden, and picked him up. I had no trouble as he was obviously used to people. She put him in a cat basket and took him away. I suppose that it was inevitable what happened next.

A man came to our front door and asked if we had seen their ginger cat and I had to explain to him what we had done. He called the animal protection people and they brought his ginger cat back. However, within a couple of days the cat was back in our garden again. He used to sit at the top of the garden looking down at our house. After a while he got more adventurous and came closer. We began to realise that he was calling for our big black cat who we called Sooty. By now he actually came down to the cat flap and cried. He was calling our cat to go out to see him.

When our cat did go out they used to kiss on the lips. It was amazing really because they were both male cats. This went on for several months until there was a time when he didn't turn up. After a while when I saw Ann, his owner, I said to her, "I haven't seen Oscar lately."

She replied, "I'm afraid that he has died".

Our cat Sooty watched out of the window for several months until he died. They were both about 10 years old., but it really was a love match. So I asked Ann if she could let us have a photo of Oscar in a frame and we would get one of Sooty, and we'd put them side by side in our bookcase and in that way they would still be together.

Snow clearing

Emily, Les and his parents at Les's niece's wedding at
Hollington Church

Chapter Nine
Amherst Gardens
and Alexandra Park

While I was working at White Rock Gardens the Deputy Superintendent came through the gardens and said to me, "How would you like to work at Amherst Gardens? The chap has been there for some time but we would like to move him to somewhere else. First of all, though, we want someone to take it over who knows what they are doing." I didn't know Amherst Gardens very well but I imagined that it was a quiet place.

So I said to him, "What about if I have a *proviso* for six months. If at that time I want to have a move back here to White Rock Gardens would that be possible?"

"Yes, I should think so," he replied.

So I spoke to Frank, the foreman of White Rock Gardens, as he had always treated me fairly and he said, "Well, it's up to you Les, if you want to go to give it a try I won't stand in your way. Likewise if you want to come back you are welcome to".

So the following week I made a start on the Monday at Amherst Gardens. Of course the first thing I did was to have a tour around the gardens, just to get the feel of the place. There was quite a lot to do generally but I think that really the main objective was the grass tennis courts. Now it was almost the end of the season and there were a lot of bare patches on the courts. So I started to cut out all the bare patches which would have to be re-laid. The next day when the general foreman came to see me I said to him that there was a lot of cutting out to do.

"Do you think someone could come and help me

by just collecting the old turf and carrying it down the steps for me, ready to be picked up by the tractor?"

"Yes I should think so, Les," he said, "I'll see if I can arrange it within a day or two."

So I thanked him and off he went. I thought that it would be a very quiet place to work and I wasn't wrong. Apart from the general foreman who came to see me I only saw two people all day.

The next day when I was walking up from the town, I saw this quite large animal coming towards me along the pavement. Just before he got to me I realised that it was a badger. It was only a little way from me when it suddenly dived into somebody's front garden. I don't know which of us was most surprised, the badger or me.

The general foreman called during the morning in his van and he had brought up some help. That was good, so I thanked him and away he went. My new mate's name was Mark and I thought to myself, 'I do hope he makes a mark'. At least he was someone to talk to.

I had to cut out a lot of the old turf and my mate would clear it up and carry it down the steps. There were many loads to bring down those steps for the tractor to pick up. I carried on cutting them out and Mark took the old turf away. It seemed to be working alright and this went on for over a week. Eventually we seemed to have cleared out the tennis courts and a tractor turned up to take the turfs away. Now we wanted some fine weather to lay the new turfs. It seemed as though the weather had changed so there might be a bit of a hold up before we could order them.

There were plenty of other jobs to do in the garden, as over the next couple of weeks we had a lot of rain. One day we had a visit from the Superintendent and he asked how I was getting on with turfing the tennis courts. I told him that I hadn't ordered the turfs yet with all this wet weather.

"How many do you need?" he asked me.

"About 1,000," I said, "but as soon as the weather improves I'll order them."

"Alright, I'll leave it to you," he agreed.

All of a sudden the weather turned fine. So I ordered the turfs and they said that they would deliver them the following day. We unloaded them between the three of us. That took some time. The next day Mark started to carry the turfs up the steps and place them as near as possible to where they had to go. So I was kept pretty busy now. Of course I couldn't lay them as fast as they were brought to me. But after a few days my mate Mark wasn't able to stay there as he was taken away to another job. So I said to him, "Just bring them up to the courts Mark and I shall have to move them from there". He brought them up as near as he could without getting in my way too much and then it was left to me.

Ironically, the Deputy Superintendent called in the next day to see how things were going and he asked me how many turfs I had to lay now. I said about 60. He said, "Well, you've got going very well and you've made a good job of it".

"Thank you," I replied, "but as it is such a quiet area here and I usually only see two or three people a day I would like to move back to White Rock Gardens when my six months are up."

"Okay, I've made a note of that," he said.

So when the time was up and I went back to my usual job, I felt quite pleased that I had made a go of it. I was even praised by the Deputy Superintendent and that was very rare. Most of my jobs were just maintenance now but they were still interesting. I teamed up with my mate George again and it was nice to be able to work together for a while.

I didn't have much time to wonder what would come next as Frank, our foreman at White Rock Gardens, said, "it seems that you have got a posting to the Park, Les, and you start there on Monday morning". I thought to myself, here we go again, but I must carry on regardless this time and not have any histrionics.

So on Monday morning I set out for Alexandra Park and I soon found out that I was needed to go motor mowing through the park with another chap. We started at the park gates and mowed the big lawn. Next we went to what is known as the Memorial bank. This is opposite the bowling green. As the time of the year was getting on we used to find a certain amount of leaves falling on the lawn. This made things more dodgy if it was wet because the leaves used to clog up the rollers of the mower and caused it to slide down the bank. I know one day particularly the rollers of my motor mower got clogged up with leaves and the mower sort of slewed around and I had a very difficult job to hold it.

We were sliding down towards where there is a shelter opposite the bowling green and we were fighting to stop it going into the shelter. After all, that shelter was meant for people to sit in, not motor mowers. After I had mowed that lawn a couple more times I got used to it.

The next lawn that we had to mow was the big lawn where they hold the Race for Life every year. We didn't have to pick up the grass as two gardeners with a barrow were picking it all up behind us. Then there was a lawn just around the corner past by the Parks Offices. The tennis courts near the crossroads where you get into the second part of the park were mowed once a week on Fridays and the bowling green was mowed three mornings a week.

The bowling green wasn't the same as other lawns.

103

Whereas you had to mow an ordinary lawn up and down, with a bowling green it had to be mown from corner to corner. The reason for this was that if the bowling green was mown just up and down the wood or bowl would be following the line of the mower. It was quite difficult to get used to it and it took a little while but once you had mastered it, it was comparatively easy. The rose garden and the flower garden were usually mown once a week just before the weekend.

While I was working in the park we had a union meeting and it was suggested that we go in for a bonus scheme. At the meeting two people were picked out and I was quite surprised when one of the names mentioned was mine. The person or persons who were going to represent the others needed two skills basically; they should be able to speak up and also be good at figures. I thought that I could do both so I allowed my name to go forward.

When we went out to make a study of these bonuses we would go with one of these people who did the job professionally. There were two of them. Before we actually worked out all the jobs and how the money was going to be increased they allowed us a certain amount of extra money. Then, the system was worked out on what they called 'factors'. A factor represented a time of 15 minutes. For instance, if you did a job in one hour that represented four factors. The maximum that you could get was 25% of your wages. So it was really worth working for. I know that some of the gardeners were dubious about it.

One day I was in the park with one of these so-called experts and I had a stop-watch on this particular person and he came striding over to me and more-or-less accused me of fraternizing with the enemy. I tried to point out to him that it should work out alright and you could get up to 25% of your wages extra. He more-or-less said that he didn't think that it would be possible. His idea was that we would have to rush around all day to get the job done quicker for the benefit of the firm.

I told him that he had a misconception if he thought that was going to happen. You certainly wouldn't have to rush around like that. If you were mowing, for instance, you got 100% for that as you were governed by the mower. If you were mowing all the time that must be 100% as you couldn't mow any quicker. However, say you stopped and had a conversation with someone for several minutes you couldn't get a maximum then because you wouldn't be mowing all the time. The only allowance that would be made would be to empty your grass box. However if you just carried on straightaway you would get 100% as it would be within your actual mowing time.

The charts showed how the factors were measured (each factor representing a quarter of an hour). Say, for instance, you were hoeing a flower bed which had an allowance of two hours, ie. eight factors, and you managed to do it in an hour and a half, you would actually have gained two factors.

It was possible to get as many as 160 factors in a week. If you could achieve this you would get your 25% bonus. Of course nothing is easy to work out, especially in its infancy. However if you worked things out properly there was a good chance that you could get the full bonus. For instance, if you were clearing the rubbish from a flower bed and it was extra rubbishy it would be best to mention it to the foreman and he would allow you extra time to get it done. This would count as unmeasured time which would go towards your other jobs, allowing you more time to do this job. There were bound to be slip-ups on some jobs which would need to be ironed out.

One job that I used to do quite regularly was when anyone wanted any tables and chairs for a function. They used to contact the Parks office. We used to keep these items in a big shed at the bottom of the park, near the gates. It was more like a warehouse than a shed. I always used to get that job for the various functions. I don't know why they chose me, unless I was the only one who could count. But I didn't mind doing it and I always had a mate to help me.

This was classed as unmeasured work because it was one of the jobs that was impossible to measure. We also had to go to collect the tables and chairs afterwards and bring them back. Well, we couldn't very well leave them there could we.

I worked mainly in the area of the park near the bandstand. Where the café is now, there were some sheds up a little slope; one where we kept the mowers and tools, and another where we went for dinner. It was rather odd really because although there were four of us who worked in that area the other three chaps went home to dinner so I was on my own. But I wasn't really alone as I had a little friend who came in the shed to see me. He was a squirrel and as I sat in the doorway he used to come into the shed and put his paws on my knee. I didn't realise what sharp little claws they have, although I suppose they need them, the way they climb up those trees.

One job that we had to deal with concerned the aviary near the café and bandstand. Someone seemed to think that it would be a good idea to cut the wire netting and let all the birds out. Most of them were budgies which I think are mainly home birds. However, about 30 escaped. We could see a number of them on the branches nearby.

We had two doors into the aviary. When we went through the outside door we used to close it before we went through the inside door to prevent the birds getting out. On this occasion we had to leave the outside door open, to try and entice them to go in on their own. It was surprising how many people closed that outside door as they went past. They probably through that we had left it open accidentally. We kept explaining to them what had happened. But we were very lucky in getting nearly all of the birds back, while we patched up the hole in the wire netting.

I was surprised one morning when I arrived for work at about 7.20. On the small lawn in front of the bowling green a meerkat was sitting, bolt upright, looking at me. He stood there for a minute and we just looked at each other. I hadn't ever seen a meerkat before, only on television. But there was no doubt in my mind that it really was a meerkat. I should think that he must have escaped from somewhere. The next morning when I walked through the park I was surprised to see him in exactly the same spot. He just sat there quite placidly looking at me. But after that I didn't see him anymore.

In the summer months we used to have fireworks in the evenings while it was quite light. We used to finish our usual job in the park half an hour earlier than usual, at about 4.00 instead of 4.30. Then we got back to the park at 5.30. There was quite a lot to do in preparation, for five of us. We assisted the chap who let the fireworks off by getting all the set pieces into position and moving things around for him.

One of us had the job of setting off the banger at the start of the session. We only did this once over the five weeks because it could be a bit dangerous, as it only had a short fuse.

When it was my turn one of the other chaps offered to do it for me. But as I had been firing shells from a 6" gun that fired 100lb shells I didn't think that I would have much trouble - admittedly that was a few years previously.

When I went to light it, part of the fuse broke off which didn't allow me much time between my lighting it and the explosion. However, it turned out to be quite safe. By the time we got home it was 11.00 at night, and we received about £2.50 extra which was quite good money in those days.

On one occasion I had a very rough night and I didn't feel very good about going to work. Anyway, I went and a job came out of the blue that only used to get done about twice a year. That was a grass bank behind the pavilion where the booking for the tennis courts was done, or anyone wanting to go onto the putting green. This bank was on the St. Helen's Road side and it stretched right up the Park Cross Road. This road separated the two parks. We went over to the bank and my two mates looked at the swops as though they had never seen one before.

The main thing to remember was to keep the swop nice and sharp otherwise it wouldn't be able to cut the grass. So that was an additional job that I had. As well as sharpening my own swop I had all three to do. Anyway, we sharpened all three and were ready to cut the grass - or so I hoped.

So I said to one of them to cut the grass first along the bottom of the bank, then gradually move farther up the bank, and bring the grass down onto the grass that has already been cut. This seemed to be quite straight-forward, or so I thought.

When I looked at him about ten minutes later he was up at the top of the bank where the grass hadn't been cut and he was moving it down the bank on to the grass that hadn't been cut. I thought that I spoke clearly enough, but apparently he didn't think so. I must admit that I was glad when 4.30 came and I was able to get out of it for a while.

The next morning I had a different mate and he was able to use a swop. It's amazing how much better we got on. It certainly was a lot more interesting and the time seemed to go quicker. So we were able to get the job done better, and in less time.

Mowing in Alexandra Park, 1967

Springtime in Alexandra Park

Miss D. Ede, Manor
Barn W.I. Judges

Les watering at Lauriston

Above: Les with Tommy the cat at Lauriston Nursing Home
Below: Les mowing with the new ATCO mower at Lauriston

Left: Les and Emily
on the seafront

Below: Les and Emily
at Old Town Week

Chapter Ten
Illness Strikes

During the autumn of 1982 I had begun to get tired when working. The week after swopping the bank, three of us had to go out on what they called 'street mowing'. This was all over the Park Estate, nearly up to the Ridge. It was very tiring and I must admit that I struggled to last the day.

I went to the doctor's that evening and he said that I was on the edge of a nervous breakdown. There are plenty of people who are ready to give you advice, usually people who haven't got a clue.

I was off work for about six weeks with the instruction 'not to worry': if I didn't worry I would be alright. How clever of them to know that. While I was at home I sat about reading, hoping to get some energy back. Then I started going out on little walks, gradually walking a little further each time, trying to get some strength back. It was an awful feeling. When I went to see my doctor after six weeks he gave me a note to say that I mustn't go out mowing the highways and byways, as my body wasn't up to it.

When I did start back to work I felt quite uneasy and I wasn't able to do very much. One day the chap who looked after the bowling green was a bit behind. The green always had to have all the moisture taken off the lawn first with a drag broom that was a yard wide, before mowing.

As I was doing this he accused me of trying to get his bonus. I said to him, "I don't want your bonus. I just thought I'd help if I could. All I want is to get through the day". I suppose that has always been my trouble, I've always been ready to help someone else, to my own detriment.

Anyway, I was put on tidying up the flower beds near to the bandstand. There were four flower beds on each corner, and including the flower bed on the bandstand itself, making five. So I was fairly happy on this job, just jogging along, not worrying about the bonus too much. I was just trying to keep going steadily. Of course this didn't please everyone I suppose. A few days later, just as I was beginning to feel better, the deputy foreman came charging down in the van one morning and said to me, "Jump in the van, Les, I am just going to pick up a couple more chaps and you're going out mowing".

"I'm sorry," I replied, "but I'm not coming as I'm not fit enough. I'll do any other job you want me to do but my doctor has given me a ticket to say that the body won't stand it. I've got the ticket in my jacket, so if you like to give it to the Deputy Superintendent I would be pleased."

He took the ticket from me and got in the van and drove off. Later in the day he came back and gave me my ticket, but he didn't tell me what had happened. I knew very well that the bosses wouldn't take it just like that.

A few weeks later the general foreman came down to pick me up and take me to the office, to see fair play. We arrived and the whole crux of the matter was that as I hadn't been able to do the job that was required of me I would be given three months' notice.

I realised that in view of my 28 years' service that I was going to do alright financially. I did feel quite bitter about it because before my illness I hadn't had a day's sickness in the last 11 years.

I left at a good time of the year on August 20th, 1982, when I was 51 years old. I had another 14 years before I could retire at 65. When we got back, Colin, the general foreman, said to me, "When I realised what was going on I expected you to explode".

I said to him, "No, I was following the proceedings and I realised that I would do very well financially".

We had a little get-together in the park on the Friday afternoon when I left. Roy, the deputy foreman, asked me, "When will you be starting work then Les?" to which I replied, "Well, I shall be starting at 8.00 Monday morning". I had written about 30 postcards and put them in newsagents and Post Offices, and I had received at least two dozen replies.

Chapter 11
Lauriston Nursing Home
and Other Gardens

I started off in the Clive Vale area, near to where we lived. I only worked for a five-hour day, 8.00-1.00 for six days a week, making a 30-hour week. I realised that the weather might not be fine all the time but the date was only August 20th so it was a good time of the year to get established.

To start off with I did my five hours in the morning and I spent most of the afternoons sorting out any other jobs. I didn't take on any that were too far away as it would take too long to get there. Also, some jobs were so small that it wouldn't have been worthwhile. I didn't turn down any job because it was too overgrown, as long as it wasn't too far away.

One job that I was able to go back to was Tower Road West as I had worked there several times before. In fact at one time I used to go there every week.

John, the owner, told that that his niece was coming down to stay for a few days. So when I went there in the morning I rang the bell at 8.00, although I had my key. A young lady came to the door. I said, "I'm sorry to disturb you but I'm the gardener. I have got my key but I didn't know what your Uncle had told you about me, but I thought that it would be best to let you know that I was here. If you had heard someone moving about in the house you may have been startled."

"No, he did tell me that you were coming, but that was very thoughtful of you," she said.

I was able to take on several more jobs and when I had been going on like this for about three years I bumped into a chap at Silverhill who I used to work with at White Rock Gardens. He had been retired for several years and he had a gardening job at a nursing home. He said that as his wife was ill he would have to pack up this job and would I be interested in taking it on. I said that I would and I would call in to see him on Friday when he came to hand out the wages.

It wasn't far away form Tower Road West, so on Friday I told John and slipped out for half an hour. I only charged him for 4½ hours and not my usual 5.

I met the treasurer at Lauriston Nursing Home and we walked around the garden together. As we walked past the conservatory I saw a cat inside. I said to him, "Oh, I see you have a cat then."

"Yes, but he won't have anything to do with you because they are all ladies here."

However, when I went to work at the nursing home, on the second day I was there I was sitting on one of the benches having my lunch and, when I looked, Tommy the cat was curled up on the seat near me. The cook told me on Monday morning that Tommy kept roaming around the garden looking for me. The cook lived in a cottage in the grounds.

I didn't realise it but there was another gardener who worked at Lauriston for two mornings a week. He was retired and he was very short. I soon found that he preferred to work on his own. Well, that was alright, I could go along with that, as far as possible.

For a while I wasn't able to fit in 20 hours a week as I had one or two other jobs to sort out. I took on one in Fearon Road for a man called Mr Duly.

He really wanted me to go each week because there was motor mowing to do, but I could only go now and then. After I had been working for Mr Duly for a few weeks I said to him that during the war when I used to go to the school at Ore village I had a school teacher by the name of Mr Duly. Would he be any relation to him? He replied, "Not only that but I am him".

I used to go there for five hours one morning a week. When I had been there for a while he went on holiday for a couple of weeks and left me with the front door key so that I was able to go in and make myself a cup of tea, which I thought was very trusting of him. The only trouble was it was quite a long walk to and fro. It was probably about a mile each way and the buses wouldn't have been very kind to me. Anyway, I'd got the lawn under control and some of the flower beds at the front.

When he came home from holiday I told him how the walk made me tired and I might have to pack it up. "Oh dear," he said, "well, I shall have to make it easier for you. I could pick you up in my car at 8.00 in the morning and then take you home at 1.00."

I was quite surprised that he was prepared to do that, but we carried on like that for a while until the end of the season.

In the back garden he had hedges each side and across the top of the garden. The following week I got the electric shears out and was cutting the hedge across the top of the garden. When I saw Mr Duly I said, "I'm cutting this hedge in preference as this is the easiest one to cut and as I haven't used one for a number of years. I can gradually get used to the machine on this one first."

Mr Duly said, "Well, that's a good idea and then it will gradually come back to you".

"I'll try to get the other two hedges done in the next two weeks." So I actually did that after I had mowed the big lawn at the back. Then as we had got to October I said to him, "That is the last one for this year".

Mainly I was trying to concentrate on my main job at the nursing home at Lauriston. I was trying to fit in as much time as possible there as it was a big garden and there was such a lot to do.

When my boss came up to Lauriston I said to him that we needed a new motor mower as the one we'd got kept breaking down. "You'll be spending money on repairs all the time and losing time on it as well."

He replied, "Next Friday when I come to pay the staff I'll take you to Mozley's and we'll pick out a mower". So when Friday came we went to the town centre to choose one. When I suggested an Atco motor mower he said, "If that's the one you think then Les that's the one we'll have, after all you are the one who's got to drive it". They delivered it within a few days.

I thought, right, perhaps we shall be able to make an improvement. So I mowed the lawn at a time when my new mate Ron wouldn't be there. I did know him very well but I knew that he would want to show me how to drive it, probably thinking that he knew more about it than I did. When he came to work the next day I told him what a good mower it was.

I was just about getting down to doing my 20 hours each week. The garden needed it as it was so large. One of the biggest jobs was the hedges which were overgrown and I realised that I would have to do a lot of secateurs work as they were too overgrown for the electric. So that would take some time.

Ron used to come for two morning a week and I was going for four mornings of five hours.

Ron had a great big wooden barrow which, with him being rather on the short side, he had a job to see over the top of, especially when it was loaded up. So I cut a lot of the hedge near the front entrance and even though I hadn't asked Ron to come and pick it up that was what he did. I thought was rather a nice gesture. I think really that it was something to do with his liking to trundle his barrow about. Anyway I was satisfied to get that part done. Ron used to leave at 12.00 but I used to work until 1.00. One area that was very overgrown was a border of six or seven hydrangeas not far from the rubbish dump. When Ron was back on the same morning as me I said, "I'm going to have a small fire each morning first thing, for about half an hour and then I shall gradually let it out." After all, we didn't want to upset the neighbours. So each morning we burnt up some rubbish and gradually got it out of the way.

When I saw Mr Robins on Friday when he came to pay us, I told him that the framework of the rose arch was rotting away and suggested that he think about getting it replaced. "If you are agreeable I'll order from French's just down the road." Of course he was in agreement as Lauriston had an account there. They were very accommodating as they sent the wood up in just over a week.

Two of us were needed on that particular job. When they delivered the wood we started taking the old wood down. A lot of it had rotted, so it didn't take much to knock it down. I said to Ron, "Would you take the old wood to somewhere near the fire?"

It was rather more tricky putting up the new framework for the roses. But I thought the residents would probably like it and it would flower that much better. I think that flowers have got minds, the same as humans. Anyway, it looked quite nice when we had finished it, even though I say so myself.

One thing about this job was that there was always work of some sort to do, regardless of the weather. Even when it was raining I sometimes went to the nursery and picked out the packets of seeds for the next year. Also, tomato plants in the greenhouse needed tying up or picking.

There is no way that we were up with the work because we were always chasing about 10 jobs. With a garden this size there would always be something to do. Now that we had the framework up for the roses I made my next job to sort out the roses and tie them up.

Then I started to cut all the hedges outside on the footpath. There certainly was a lot to cut. After I'd got a little way in front Ron appeared with his big barrow. I decided to leave the hedge until the Wednesday so that Ron would be able to shift it then. On Tuesday, I just did a bit of tidying up. As I hoped, on Wednesday Ron was there with his big barrow. It's not as though I was expecting him to do the collection of the rubbish but I was pretty sure that he would.

Outside the front at Lauriston there was a big flower bed containing a lot of shrubs. There was a gravel path and about three large rocks at the front of the flower bed with the idea of keeping the cars off the bed. When I saw the postman I spoke to him about someone taking one of the rocks. I was very surprised when he told me that when he sat on the wall at Maze Hill waiting for his second delivery of mail he wasn't able to do that now. When I asked him why, he said that someone had taken the whole wall. It was very difficult to understand how they could do such a thing.

Now we were beginning to get the front part of the garden tidy. I pruned the shrubs that were in the front bed. I hadn't been out there very long when I got my finger too close to the blade of the secateurs and it certainly did bleed. I rushed into the kitchen and wrapped a towel around it but it was soaked in no time. It was a good job there was a visitor who had a car. He took me down to the casualty department of East Sussex Hospital, which isn't there now.

When they cleaned it off and put something on to reduce the pain it was still very painful and I'm sure that I hit my head on the ceiling. They also gave me an anti-tetanus jab and then I went home. It was past my working time so I didn't return to Lauriston that day.

I can see why it was so painful, as I'd actually cut the tip of my finger off. It was difficult to imagine that I cut all those hedges out the front with my secateurs and there were no problems.

When I went into work the next day I was interrogated by Ron who asked how I managed to cut my finger like that. I had no answer really. The only answer I could give was that I wasn't paying as much attention as I should have been. It really was difficult to do much in the way of gardening. I had just to do a little bit here and there and hope that it soon improved. We had the weekend inbetween so it gave me some little time to begin to get over it.

When Monday came I had a look at where we had the fires and I hoped to be able to cut up some of that rubbish for burning. That was one of the few things that I could do but I would have to be especially careful. Apart from that all I was able to do was to supervise which didn't do much for me.

I think that it was a question of time. My recovery went on for several weeks where I just had to do what I could. It was even a bit difficult to get the mowing done. It did take me a lot longer than it did before as I had to be very careful that I didn't knock that hand. It was still very sore so I just had to do jobs that didn't require too much effort.

I asked Ron if he would swop the grass outside and so away he went. He cut the grass alright and raked it all up and brought it in. But when I went round to have a look he had left a swop outside in the middle of the footpath. It was a good thing that a child didn't get hold of it.

I know that I was a bit haphazard at working out the work arrangements but for the time being anyhow I had to do what I could.

I managed to get the rose beds edged up, weeded and hoed. Things were looking up now and I was very gradually making progress. One of the biggest beds to be sorted out was the large herbaceous border. It was the same size as a cricket wicket, 22yds in length and about 8ft wide. There was certainly plenty of rubbish to come out of that bed.

Things were picking up now and we were winning. We had a wet morning on the Thursday so I spent most of the time in the greenhouse. I was hoping to mow the lawn next Monday because on Tuesday there was a coffee morning. Anyway, the weather was good and we had quite of lot of people come. I think very often it was the same people who came. There were occasions when they included some dancing girls. There was plenty of room to hold such things.

On the grapevine we heard that one or two of the residents of Lauriston were leaving to go into other nursing homes. The problem would be that if there were too few residents Lauriston would have to close. The following week we were given a talk by the manager who told us that it was possible that Lauriston might close. Apparently it was on the cards that it was for sale. Ron had retired and I was the only one working in the garden now.

I was expecting to go into the Conquest Hospital for a prostate operation. My boss came up to Lauriston on Wednesday and told me that the nursing home had indeed been sold. I said to him, "That's handy, I have got to go into the Conquest on Sunday for a prostate operation". He said that he would collect the keys on Friday. I said, "This has put me in a hole. I'll not be able to do any heavy work for about six weeks after the operation".

The operation would be on September 11th, 1994. I popped in at No. 32 Tower Road West to see John and he said that when I was fit I could go back to my five hours a week there. I also asked my boss at Lauriston if he could get in touch with the new people and maybe get me to carry on looking after the garden for a time, otherwise it would soon get overrun with weeds. So he said that he would do that.

I went into the Conquest on Sunday 10th September in the afternoon. Several of us were sat in a row, waiting. I was situated right opposite a clock. I thought how ideal, at least I shall know the time.

The next day, as they were wheeling me down the corridor I was a bit dopey but I remember saying, "Well, if you would only let me know which way you are going I'll put out my appropriate arm". I didn't seem to know much after that until I came round on the ward.

There were only six of us on the ward, three each side. There was a chap opposite to me and he kept having a bit of a cross talk to me. One day he must have seen that my name was Catt, which was above my bed. He said, "If you don't leave off I shall take you down to the vet's".

So later on when he was talking to the chap in the next bed to him and saying that at the shop at Hollington you couldn't ask for the wrong thing. So I came back with the remark, "It's a pity you don't ask for some brains then".

I was only there for another couple of days and my wife came up to fetch me in a taxi. "Oh, thank you very much for taking him home," said the chap. I shook hands with the staff and the other patients. Just before I left there the surgeon came over to me and warned that for a while I would experience a little blood coming away, so to be ready for that.

I got home and settled in but in a day or two I started to go out, gradually at first and then a little further each day to try and get stronger.

I received a letter from my boss at Lauriston,

saying that once I was fit enough they would like me to carry on working at Lauriston for four hours, two days a week, making eight hours a week. They would send me a cheque each week.

When I was a bit fitter I went up to Tower Road West to see John. The dog came over and put his head on my knee. He was a spaniel and he liked plenty of fuss but I don't know how he knew it was me as he had gone blind. I was pretty annoyed when I was told that the cleaning woman had left the door of the cellar open and he had fallen down the steps. What sort of person would leave a door open to a cellar, knowing there is a blind dog in the house.

When I had got back to Lauriston I had a little walk down to French's nursery to see if they ever heard of any gardening work.

I arranged with John to go up to Tower Rd West one morning a week for five hours. Combined with Lauriston, I had 13 hours' work a week so far.

I used to have some arguments with John but neither of us fell out with the other as we respected one another.

He was a big man with a big heart but his health wasn't so good. Once a year he used to get the big bands together and they used to meet at a pub near Battle and I think that they had quite a jam session.

One morning I was walking past the nursery when one of the chaps from there said, "As you asked me about another gardening job, I have got one for you just around the corner, 58 Sedlescombe Road South".

I went up to see the lady straightaway. I explained that I had just had an operation but I should be alright to make a start in about four weeks. While I was there I looked around the garden. It was quite big and untidy but not like some that I had seen. We agreed the price and I said that I would ring her up the evening before I made a start. The only other thing I had to say was that I would be finishing my gardening on April 2nd as I would be 65 on that day.

I got back to Lauriston and picked up the keys. All the furniture had gone now and it was very cold inside. In fact I went into the garage and had my lunch. I liked to go in through the front door, but the alarm went off and I had to reset it.

I went in one morning and I remember that it was wet. I walked through to the back door and I saw all these footprints in the hall. They were wet but very difficult to understand. In fact they were quite creepy. When I phoned my guvnor he said there was a break-in and the police came in with their dogs. No wonder it was a bit creepy. Although I'm not the most scared person that there is, I was certainly a bit on edge until I knew what had caused it.

One other morning I saw that they had bashed several windows in at the back. So I called at the house next door to ask them if I could phone up my guvnor. I had known them for all the time I had worked at Lauriston, about 9½ years, so they were only too pleased to help.

When I got through to him on the phone he seemed very nonchalant about it, but said that I must always check around the outside before I went in. A few days after that they went up the fire escape and went into a room at the top and stole a clock.

I was working for eight hours each week at Lauriston now. They sent me a cheque once a month and I wrote to them when I got it. I also worked for another five hours at Tower Road, that made 13, and then two mornings at 58 Sedlescombe Road South, which was another eight hours, making a total of 21 hours each week. I thought, "Oh well, that will take me up to my 65th birthday on April 2nd".

There were certainly a lot of thoughts going through my mind about the way things had gone over the years. I could not realise that my 51 years as a professional gardener were finally coming to an end. I must admit that I had mixed feelings. There were so many things that had gone on over that time, some of them good and some of them bad.

There was a lot of work to do at 58 Sedlescombe Road South. It wasn't in such a bad state as some gardens that I had had to deal with. It was quite a big garden, but one good thing about it was that it was the time of year when the weeds wouldn't be growing much. When I felt a little better I worked for another four hours one morning, making it three mornings, and in total 25 hours a week.

I actually worked on April 2nd, my 65th birthday, and stopped the following day. Still, why not? I had also worked on my 14th birthday which made it 51 years to the day. Except if you take out my two years of National Service.

I must say that I worked with some top blokes and I enjoyed their company and their wisecracks enormously. I'm afraid that a lot of them are not with us today, but I do still think of them.

I did feel very off about someone's thoughts when I was working with him in Gensing Gardens. I can honestly say that in the whole of my working life of 51 years never at any time did I expect anyone to do my work for me. In fact, as well as keeping my part of the job done I very often helped others by doing their share of the work as well. So to be castigated in this way was very hurtful to me. Anyone that knew me would vouch for me.

Once I had retired I could at last just look after one garden. My own. Also, I was able to put my feet up at last. I started going out for long walks as I have always liked walking. I always wore my heavy boots as I found them better for my feet.

One morning, when I had almost finished my

walk, I stopped at Mount Road Post Office to get our two pensions, mine and my wife's. The two ladies who work behind the counter seemed to be having a debate about something. So I walked down Mount Road and round the very quiet corner of Edmund Road.

As I did so, two young fellows jumped me. I then realised what the debate was about at the Post Office. Apparently they were talking about these two fellows who were opposite the Post Office and they evidently thought that they were suspicious-looking characters. I think that it would have been better if they had told their suspicions to other people in the Post Office.

I got thrown on the ground and I got a good kicking in the ribs. As I had my heavy boots on I managed to get one or two kicks in myself. However, it's not very easy if you try to kick someone when you are lying on the ground. Just at that moment a car came down Edmund Road sounding the hooter. The two fellows soon made off round the corner. The car owner, a lady, asked me where I lived, helped me into her car and took me home.

Soon after I got home a police constable called to take a statement. He was there for about 1½ hours. I told him that I managed to get a couple of kicks in while I was lying on the ground and he said, "Good for you". However, if I had picked up a brick and hit them with it I would be held responsible.

I didn't return to that area for a long time. But one morning I was walking up the High Street in the old town when I heard someone running up the pavement behind me. I turned rather quickly as I was still a bit nervy. When I turned round I saw that it was a young girl of about 20. She was sorry to have startled me, but I explained, "It's not your fault. I was attacked by two men about three weeks ago and I am still a bit nervy".

There was something else that was quite a nasty

jolt to my wife and I. It happened at about 1.45am one Christmas morning several years ago, when we lived in Harold Road. I am a very heavy sleeper but there was a terrible crash on our front door as someone was kicking it. I said to my wife, "Don't put the light on or draw the curtains". This chap had got fed up with kicking the door and had now started on kicking the windows. It was a good job they had been double-glazed. After calling the police they arrived very quickly. The chap who was kicking said that he was looking for his parents. It's a funny way to look for them by trying to kick the door in. When I spoke to one of the policemen on the phone and asked if he was going to arrest him, he said, "No, we can't do that as he hasn't committed any crime".

One afternoon when the weather was nice and warm my wife and I went for a walk over the East Hill. When we got up there, there was a cricket match going on. Just off the pitch where they were playing there were several areas of long grass. When I went over closer I saw that there was a snake curled up. I didn't think that it was a grass snake. So I mentioned this to a couple of officials who were nearby. One of them picked it up and was bitten by it. The next thing we knew an ambulance had turned up and taken him to the Conquest. He went straight into the intensive care department. Luckily they saved him, but it was touch and go. Why do people do such silly things?

I heard that they were intending to knock down the existing building at Lauriston, and were going to rebuild it, replacing it with a 60-bed nursing home. I thought that I would like to attend the grand opening by the Mayor. As I had been working at Lauriston for about 10½ years I still held a strong interest in the building. I received a nice letter back saying that my wife and I would certainly receive an invitation from the Mayor, and true to their word we did.

When the day came, anybody who was anybody was there and it was a great buffet tea. I don't know how it happened but my wife and I were almost the first in the queue. On the way back we saw Michael Foster MP and his wife in the queue. So I said to him, "I bet you don't have to queue up like this in the House of Commons do you Michael?" to which he replied, "No, we don't." I told him that I remembered when he used to play the trumpet in the band. He said that he still played now and again. So I told him that I used to play a musical instrument when I was a young boy. Of course he asked me what it was. So I said that I used to play on the linoleum. But he didn't think that was funny.

As we came away I felt quite sad as that was my gardening career finished. I had always tried to be helpful and never to put on my mates, but always to work my corner.

***

These days, we like to go out for short bus rides to Bexhill for dinner. We also go to Battle on a Thursday to visit some very nice gardens which are looked after by amateur gardeners for about three hours on that day. We have met these gardeners several times now and we are getting to know each other by name.

We also like to go to Rye where they do a great fish and chip dinner. We know the owner and staff quite well and over the years I have bombarded them with several of my poems (see opposite).

I also enjoy giving talks on gardening and taking the occasional walk around the parks in Hastings, where I worked for so long.

Poems

I have always enjoyed writing poetry, and a number of my poems have appeared in the *Hastings and St. Leonard's Observer*. I am reproducing some of my favourites here.

Crystal

Emmie Catt - 14.1.67-14.1.82
Although you knew when we first met,
That I always loved a bet,
You didn't realise you were my choice,
When I proposed and lost my voice.
You agreed to partner me through life,
And become my darling wife,
Through ups and down we've triumphed through,
Mainly though, because of you.
But now it should be Crystal clear,
That I hold you very dear
With your love I'll always treasure,
When I sit back at my leisure,
Because I knew no one else can measure,
And realise how much pleasure,
You've given me so much cheer,
So I thank you for 15 years.
From your loving Hubby, Les

China

Emmie Catt - 14.1.67-14.1.87
Now we celebrate our China,
But with your 20 years of caring,
Which you must have found so wearing
In all that time we've loved and won,
Which can't be said of everyone.

It hasn't always been plain sailing,
Especially when we have been ailing.
It is of course quite a test,
But for me, I got the best.
Marriage is a very long sentence,
But for me there is no repentance.
We've neither of us been a trend-setter,
And always wanting something better,
But been satisfied with our lot.
And quite happy with what we've got.
It's been a nice outlook on life,
With such an understanding wife,
And as the years just come and go,
Our love just seems to grow.
So through all our laughs and some tears,
Thank you dear, for 20 good years.
All my love always, Les

Pearl

Emmie Catt - 14.1.67-14.1.97
30 years have rushed along,
It's amazing where they have gone,
It has become as clear as a bell,
It's because we've worked together so well.
We've worked at it right from the start,
And you have always been in my heart
Through all our ups and downs
And quite a lot of worried frowns,
Sometimes we've been at the end of our tether
And although I'm getting older
My love for you will never get colder
So I must conclude with this toast
Here's to the one I'll always love the most.
Your loving hubby, Les

Ruby

Forty years have moved along
It's surprising how quickly they have gone
Some of them were difficult but most were fun
Just as they were when we first begun
There has been so little strife
As we've made the best of life
It would appear to be fiction
As there's been so little friction
But we seem to complement each other
That is why we've had so little bother
It's a pity we left it so late
But for me it was worth the wait
After all is said and done
It was destiny that you were the one
For me you were the perfect choice
Which makes me always to rejoice
And as our marriage lasts longer
My love for you grows ever stronger
From your loving hubby, always, Les.

Retirement

Emmie Catt - December 20th
Now that you have come of age,
It's time to turn another page,
You have never been one to shirk,
Through all your years at work,
But have always done your best,
So now is the time to take a rest.
You will have more time for pleasure,
And enjoy it at your leisure,
Life will be much the same,
And not in any way mundane,
You can use your half fare passes,

And maybe wear stronger glasses,
And although I'll see you longer,
My love for you gets even stronger.
Your ever loving Hubby, Les.

For A Very Special Friend -
Our Cat Jimmy Who was With Us For 16½ Years

We had a lovely cat called Jim,
And we really thought the world of him.
He had such a great loyalty,
That to us he was just like royalty.

When we sat at the table dining
He looked up at us with his eyes shining.
For his dinner we had made him wait
As we arrived home rather late.
When at last he got his reward
He went to sleep as he got bored
He seemed to sleep all day and night,
But being a cat that was his right

When he went out in the cold
He didn't seem very bold
He dashed out and dashed back
And he didn't even wear a mac

He really was a jolly good pal,
What's more he liked us as well
And when we were feeling in the dumps,
He always seemed to turn up trumps.

And early morning the stairs we did descend
There to greet us was our furry friend.

My Short Stay at the Conquest

A short while ago I came to dread
A stay in a Hospital bed
But I was greeted to my surprise
By Nurses who were very wise
And although I was there for a while
They never forgot to smile
They seemed to work with one accord
To Benefit the patients on their Ward
They put the patients at their ease
Which to them seemed to have unlimited powers
As they battled away for very long hours
And you feel that after all their toiling
It's really YOU that they are spoiling
Although it's something you have to endure
You know they are ready with a cure
And they seemed to know just how you feel
Which really is asking a very great deal
And when you're feeling rather fearful
They always make you feel very cheerful
And all the Hospital Staff
Always seem ready with a laugh
And as a tribute to the Nurses
I thought I would write these few Verses
But really it is very tough
As it would never be enough.

A Staycation

In need of a holiday, a break from dull routine,
But money's tight, with bills to pay and times are lean?
Well, I have the answer, the new 'in place' to go,
Staycation is the latest trend and expenses really low!
You know the bed is comfy,
The tea and coffee free,
A picnic in the park is fun,
Enjoy the scenery.
Relaxing in the garden with the
Book you want to read,
Burgers on the barbie and all
The ice cream you could need
Is waiting in the freezer,
Just a few steps away.
With no queues to make you grumpy
And nothing to be paid.
Yes, staycation is where I'm heading!
This summer will be great,
No travel stress, no case to pack,
I really cannot wait.

For The Park Staff

No doubt my corny gags you'll miss
But on reflection will say 'What bliss'
A voice from the corner which is like a roar
Followed by a Liverpudlian one that says
'What a bore'.
When a voice just as large
Says 'I'm in charge'
Another cuts a caper
When picking up paper
And dashing about with the speed of a tractor
Is someone looking for one more factor?
Up bobs a head, like a pixie
With hearing aid saying 'too risky'.

I must thank the staff
Who have given me a laugh
I have been rather outrageous
Which sometimes gets contagious
But I feel a little sad
And also rather glad
My time has come to finish
But my regards will not diminish
Although I may pine
I've enjoyed my time
But enough is enough
When the going is tough.